THEY "KNEW" BILLY THE KID

THE FIVE CENT
WIDE AWAKE
LIBRARY

Entered according to Act of Congress, in the year 1881, by FRANK TOUSEY, in the office of the Librarian of Congress, at Washington, D. C.

Entered at the Post Office at New York, N. Y., as Second Class Matter.

No. 451. { COMPLETE. } FRANK TOUSEY, PUBLISHER, 20 ROSE STREET, N. Y. { PRICE } Vol. I.
NEW YORK, August 29, 1881. ISSUED EVERY MONDAY. { 5 CENTS. }

THE
TRUE LIFE OF
BILLY THE KID

THEY "KNEW" BILLY THE KID

INTERVIEWS WITH OLD-TIME NEW MEXICANS

edited by
Robert F. Kadlec

with an Afterword by
Jeff Dykes
and Notes by
Marta Weigle

Ancient City Press
Santa Fe, New Mexico

International Standard Book Number:
0-941270-36-X (paper)
0-941270-37-8 (cloth)
Library of Congress Catalogue Number:
87-070295

Second Edition

Designed by Mary Powell
Cover Design by Stephen Tongier

Printed in the United States of America

Frontispiece: Cover of the 1881 dime novel by John Woodruff Lewis (Don Jenardo), *The True Life of Billy the Kid,* Wide Awake Library, Vol. 1, No. 451 (August 29, 1881). Photo courtesy Museum of New Mexico, Neg. No. 92018.

CONTENTS

PREFACE

In the late 1930s, the Federal Writers' Project (FWP) provided work for at least five thousand writers, researchers, administrators, clerks and other personnel who were victims of the Great Depression. Among those joining the ranks of the FWP were Ross Santee, John Lomax, Ray Billington, Ben Botkin, and Mari Sandoz, all of whom would later achieve success in their chosen fields.

Salaries were meager, in many cases barely subsistence wages. The New York City group was paid a little over one hundred dollars a month each, while workers in Georgia and Mississippi, for example, had to survive on about forty dollars a month.

The Project is best remembered for the tremendous work resulting in the WPA Guides to states and cities. In addition to this guide program, however, smaller regional programs were also instituted where teams of writers recorded much local history and folklore. Unfortunately, most of this never reached publication.

The material in this book evolved from such a federal and state-sponsored program. After 1942, these oral histories were placed in libraries in Santa Fe, Washington, D.C., and elsewhere. Bits of these writings have appeared occasionally in books and articles about Billy the Kid, but this is the first time that the gleanings from the New Mexico FWP files have been garnered and published together.

These stories about Billy the Kid during his heyday are the reminiscences of old-timers almost sixty years after the fact. At the time of harvesting this material, most of the raconteurs were in the sixty-to-ninety age group. It is reasonable to assume that those in a lower age bracket did not "know" Billy but remembered the tales of their elders.

A hundred years ago the citizenry of Billy-country were not subjected to a daily barrage of news from all parts of the world. Thus events of epic proportion, such as the antics of The Kid, left lasting impressions on the populace. There is no doubt that over the years the stories were embellished to suit each teller's taste, but the memories remained. Luckily, these narrations were recorded.

Through the years, Billy-experts have pointed out and "corrected" discrepancies of the Kid's doings. We have not attempted to do so here. It is our intention to present these yarns as they were told and written up. Variations in spelling of names and places and questionable syntax remain as set down by the scribes of the Writers' Project. We hope these vignettes will be of interest to Billy-buffs everywhere.

Santa Fe, New Mexico
December 15, 1986   Robert F. Kadlec

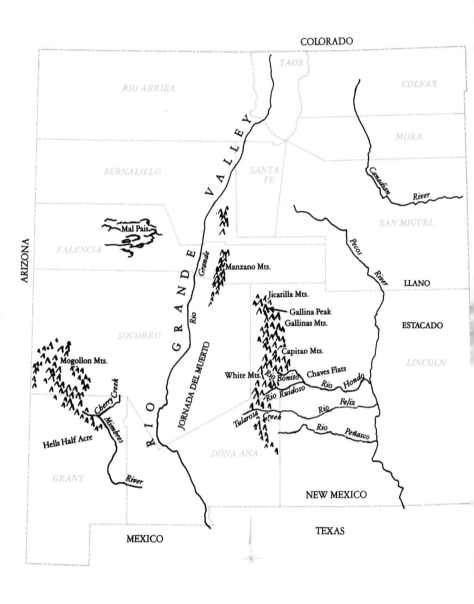

1880 New Mexico county outline map showing landforms and rivers mentioned in text..

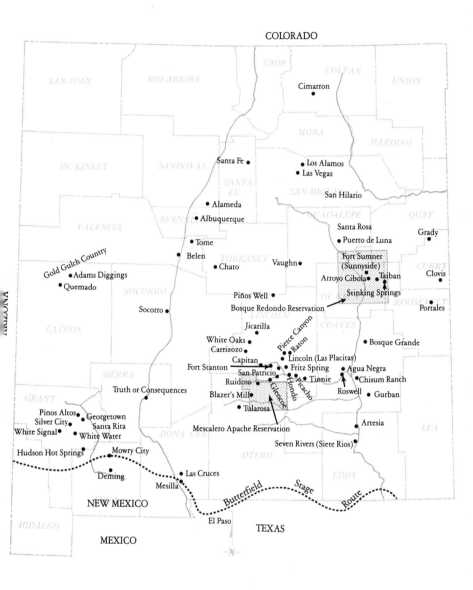

1930 New Mexico county outline map showing identifiable places mentioned in text.

►1◄

SILVER CITY DAYS
AND BILLY'S MOTHER

BILLY'S MOTHER, CATHERINE McCARTY (1829-74), married William Henry Harrison Antrim (1842-1922) on March 1, 1873, in Santa Fe. Together with her sons Henry and Joseph, they moved to Silver City. To help support the family Mrs. Antrim took in boarders. She died of consumption on September 16, 1874. The obstreperous Henry McCarty, then probably fifteen years old, was arrested and jailed on September 23, 1875, but escaped on September 25 and left Silver City for Globe, Arizona. [1]

LOUIS ABRAHAM OF SILVER CITY

COLLECTED BY MRS. FRANCES TOTTY, 1937

Mrs. Bill Antrim was a jolly Irish lady, full of life, and her fun and mischief. Mrs. Antrim could dance the Highland Fling as well as the best of the dancers.

There were very few American boys in Silver City when the Antrims lived here, therefore the few American boys that were here ran together all of the time. The Antrim house was the place where the boys gathered most of the time.

Mrs. Antrim always welcomed the boys with a smile and a joke. The cookie jar was never empty to the boys. From school each afternoon we made straight for the Antrim home to play.

My mother was dead, and my father had a Spanish woman for a cook, her food never tasted as good as the meals that Mrs. Antrim cooked. I ate many meals in the home of Billie the Kid and I know that I was welcome.

Mrs. Antrim was as good as she could be, and she made every one welcome in her home. When she died in 1873, she was buried in the City Cemetery. There was not a hearse in Silver City then so my father's Surry was used to carry the body to the cemetery.

Billie and I as well, soon learned we had lost a dear ally and friend, as well as his mother. A cousin of Mrs. Antrim came back from the East a few years ago and placed a monument at her grave.

I have often been thankful that she never had to know of the trouble Billie became involved in for it would have broken her heart. How thankful I am to know that that good woman never had to face that heartache.

Billie's home was an ordinary good American home. Good parents, and a good environment in the home. Billie's father came to Georgetown and settled. There he died.

Mr. Antrim, Billie's stepfather, was a mining man at Georgetown. Billie Bonney's mother married Mr. Antrim and the family moved to Silver City in 1870. Here Billie lived until he was arrested by Sheriff Whitehill.

The story of Billie the Kid killing a blacksmith in Silver City is false. Billie never was in any trouble at all, he was a good boy, maybe a little mischievous at times than the rest of us with a little more nerve.

When the boy was placed in jail and escaped he was not bad, he was just scared. If he had only waited until they let him out he would have been alright, but he was scared and he ran away.

He got in with a band of rustlers at Apache Tejo in the part of the county where he was made a hardened character.

Ed Moulton, a miner and friend of Mr. Antrim, was like a father to Billie for he had known the family for a long time and was in their home but Billie never did kill anyone over Mr. A. Moulton.

Mr. Antrim was a man of good character, and was highly respected here until his death. Joe Bonney, Billie's brother, left here and was thought well of until he turned gambler, and went to his death in Colorado with his boots on. These two boys of a good and happy family, good boys when they were youngsters came to a tragic end for what reason no one knows.

Billy the Kid's boyhood home on Main Street north of Broadway, Silver City, New Mexico, ca. 1880. Photo by Alfred S. Addis. Courtesy Museum of New Mexico, Neg. No. 99054.

Billie had no reason, only fear, for he hung around Apache Tejo quite a while, and Sheriff Whitehill could have gotten him if he had of wanted him punished for there was law and order in Silver City then even if sometimes the gun did speak too soon, the killer was tried.[2]

MRS. LOUIS ABRAHAM OF SILVER CITY

COLLECTED BY MRS. FRANCES TOTTY, 1937

I didn't know Billie the Kid, but my husband went to school with him. The boys and girls that knew him never thought of him as a criminal, but a boy that was full of fun and mischief. He like all other boys liked to put a snake on the teacher's desk or chase a girl with a mouse, and the other hundreds of things that fun loving mischief boys like to do. His eyes were always dancing and full of a mischievous fun.

Billie's real name was Henry McCarty. The family lived in a log house by the Big Ditch. Billie's father was dead, and after the family had been here some time Mrs. McCarty married William Antrim.

Mrs. Antrim did the town baking and was very famous for her pies and cakes.

When Billie was nine years old his mother died. Billie and a younger brother were left to the care of their step-father who was both father and mother to the boys doing all he could for them.

Billie was never in any serious trouble in Silver City. The story of Billie killing a man over insulting his mother is absolutely false. He never killed anyone in Silver City or Grant County as far as we old timers know.

He stole some money from a Chinaman in Georgetown and Harvey Whitehill the sheriff at that time arrested Billie and placed him in jail.

The jail in Silver City at that time was a crude building with a large old-fashioned fire place and chimney.

Billie, a youngster, being used to freedom and the outdoors soon became tired of the jail and desired to get out. He began to search for a means of escape. He proceeded to climb out the chimney and escaped from jail.

Billie left Grant County and never returned again, but now he was a criminal for he had escaped jail.

Billie a fun loving boy now must fight to get by in the world and was soon known as a gun-man, but we wonder if a lot of these killings aren't false as was the one of his killing in Silver City.[3]

UNNAMED SILVER CITY RESIDENT

COLLECTED BY BETTY REICH, 1937

William Bonney, better known as Billy the Kid, lived in Silver City when a very young boy with his mother, brother and step-father. The boy was an ordinary boy, though he began to get into trouble at an early age.

He worked in a butcher shop for a man by the name of Charles Bottom.

Mr. Bottom, a native of Kentucky, suffered from chills and fever. He owned a fine racing mare of which he thought a great deal.

One day a youth said to Mr. Bottom, "If you will let me take the mare, I'll go to Cherry Creek (12 or 14 miles from Silver City) and get some cherry bark and maybe it will help your chills."

Mr. Bottom told him the Indians were pretty bad and that it was dangerous.

Finally one morning he consented to let the boy take the mare and go to Cherry Creek. He returned that evening with the cherry bark. Bottom said the boy had plenty of nerve.

Later on the Kid was arrested for larceny at Mowry City, a stage stand on the old Butterfield Trail and now known as Old Town.

After that he was arrested for breaking into a Chinaman's place and stealing some shirts and other articles.

While awaiting trial in the Silver City jail he, and a man being held for an Arizona crime, broke jail. This jail was constructed of 3 × 6's and rock.

This was the beginning of the life of crime led by the young outlaw. Billy the Kid never killed a man in Silver City. It was not until he had left Silver City that he killed his first man.

After breaking jail the Kid was not heard of for some time. He had gone to Arizona and was staying with a blacksmith. It was reported that this man was very overbearing. The Kid killed him and was an outlaw from then on.[4]

DICK CLARK OF SILVER CITY

COLLECTED BY MRS. FRANCES TOTTY, 1937

"Billie the Kid was not a bad boy in his school days. The Kid, like other boys, was full of fun and deviltry, but for him killing anyone in Silver City, not hardly.

"I have talked to him many times; he was always courteous and respected his elders.

"His eyes were those of a person full of fun, he was generous and kind to everyone until someone did him dirt then he would seek revenge, which was his beginning on the road of crime.

"I never knew Billie's father; if he came to Silver City I never heard of it. The family seemed to have gotten here when Silver City was a new town for they were in Georgetown before Silver City.

"Billie's mother married Bill Antrim. Mr. Antrim was good to his stepchildren, there being two boys. Mrs. Antrim helped suupport the family by baking pastries that were sold very easily in town.

"Mr. Antrim was a good man, but he liked his liquor too well. I wonder if this didn't have some influence on the boy's life, for after his mother's death, which was probably in 1871 — I can't say for sure — the two boys were left to the care of their stepfather.

"Mrs. Antrim is buried in the old cemetery, northeast of town. I think I could take you to the grave but I'm not positive.

"I don't like to say when she died, but I know that Billie was a youngster.

"Mr. Antrim being a man highly thought of as to character was mother and father to the boys in the best way he knew how.

"After the boys left Silver City Mr. Antrim first lived one place then another. I think when he died he was living with the Snyder family north of town.

"If Mr. Antrim had any correspondence with the boys it wasn't known for he never mentioned them to anyone after they left.

"I have been told that Joe settled in South Texas and was a highly respected citizen owning quite a bit of property. He got into some trouble and left Silver City.

"As far as I know Billie was never in any trouble in Silver City until he stole from a Chinaman who had caused Billie to seek some revenge on him by some method. Harvey Whitehill, sheriff, at that time arrested Billie and placed him in the County's crude jail, crude even for those days.

"Thus began the Kid's career of crime.

"The Kid was a slim boy who could always get a laugh from any source whether the joke being on him or someone else. He evidently didn't like his lodging and as there was a fireplace in the northeast corner of the jail he thought of a better place outside.

"As I said the Kid was slim, the boy was able by some means to climb through the chimney. The boy after escaping knew he had to leave Grant County or be captured and placed in jail again.

"As Billie had no way of leaving he stole a horse and saddle, then added a pistol to his supplies and left Grant County to begin a career of crime that is well remembered by the Southwest."[5]

R. ATHON OF SILVER CITY

COLLECTED BY FRANCES E. TOTTY, 1938

Billie the Kid's career of crime was started by a kiddish prank here in Silver City, where Wells Saloon now stands is where an old log Chinese laundry at one time stood. One afternoon Billie with Louie Abhram and one or two other white boys that lived in Silver City were walking down the street and while passing the laundry a remark was made about the laundry and Billy in fun jumped over the fence and took one of the shirts off the line, but the mistake was made of the Chink saw the boy and called sheriff Whitehill, the boy was caught, and he readily admitted taking the shirt, and was placed in jail.

The boy didn't like staying jail and decided to leave the place, but he realized that if he escaped from the jail and stayed in town he would be put back in jail so he crawled out the chimney and traveled down to Apache Tejo where he fell in with a bunch of rough men rustlers and petty thieves, here the boy learned the rough ways of the desperado.

Billie the Kid didn't kill anyone in Silver City, it has been said that he killed a blacksmith at Apache Tejo, but as far as I know this fact has never been established true.

Across from here Louis Abhrams Southern Hotel now stands is where Mrs. Anthrium, Billie's mother lived in a log house and ran a boarding house for the early traveler through this part of the country. Mrs. Athrium died in Silver City and was buried in the old cemetery, one mile northeast of town. A cousin from the East some years ago erected a monument at her grave or the last resting place of the mother of New Mexico's young desperado would probably be lost.[6]

PAUL MAYER OF CARRIZOZO

COLLECTED BY EDITH L. CRAWFORD, 1937

I came to White Oaks, New Mexico, March 15, 1881, about six weeks before Billy the Kid killed Bell and Olinger at Lincoln.

At that time I was told that Billy the Kid's mother was living in Silver City, New Mexico, and he left home because he had killed a man for making insulting remarks about his mother.

My impression has always been that his mother was living during the Lincoln County War.[7]

DR. M. G. PADEN OF CARRIZOZO

COLLECTED BY EDITH L. CRAWFORD, 1937

I came to White Oaks, New Mexico, in the year of 1880, and had always been told by the old timers that Billy the Kid's mother was living when he left home and came to Lincoln County. My impression has always been that she died after he became an out-law.[8]

MRS. ANNIE E. LESNETT OF CARRIZOZO

COLLECTED BY EDITH L. CRAWFORD, 1937

It was about the time the Lincoln County War started, that I had inflammatory rheumatism, and as soon as I was able to travel my husband took me to the Hudson Hot Springs, at Silver City, New Mexico, the springs were located near the town of Silver City, so we stopped in Silver City, and met Dick Hudson, who owned and operated the springs, we staid all night at a hotel run by a Mrs. Antrim, who I found out later was Billy the Kid's mother.

Dick Hudson was asking us about the Lincoln County War while we were eating supper we told him all we knew about it.

Later on that evening Mrs. Antrim told me about her young son getting into trouble and leaving home and that she had not heard from him, and did not know where he was.[9]

COLLECTED BY EDITH L. CRAWFORD, 1937

In the spring of 1877, I went to the hot springs located near Silver City. There were no accommodations at the springs at that time so I stayed in Silver City at a hotel, run by a Mrs. Antrim. While I was there she cried and told me of her young son, of how he had come home one night and said he was leaving the country, and she fixed him up a few clothes and tied them up in a red bandana handkerchief and kissed him good bye. She had never heard from him since. She said he was such a good boy and so young to be out in the world alone.

At that time I never dreamed of this being Billy the Kid's mother, as I knew him then as William Bonney, and did not know that he came from Silver City, as in those days news was so slow getting around. Later on I found out that she was the mother of Billy the Kid. I was so sorry for her and would have liked to have told her all I knew about her son. She was so broken hearted and I could have told her so many nice things about her boy that would have comforted her. He was always so nice and polite and so considerate of women folks.

One time he came to our ranch home, his clothes were all torn and he was limping. I asked him what was the matter and he said: "I will tell you, Mrs. Lesnett, they had me in a close place, I was riding for my life and my horse ran under a tree and tore my clothes and hurt my leg pretty bad." I called the cook and told him to fix up Billy's leg while I went down to the store and got him a shirt and a pair of overalls. When Billy saw what I had done for him, he said: "God bless you, Mrs. Lesnett, I will always love you for this."[10]

COLLECTED BY EDITH L. CRAWFORD, 1937

I first knew Billy the Kid before the Lincoln County War. He was working for Mr. Tunstill. They were going over to the Feliz Ranch with a herd of horses. They stopped by our place on the Ruidoso at the Dowlins Mill and had dinner with us.

Billy the Kid came to my house many times during the Lincoln County War, and after the War while he was hiding from the officers I always fed him, when he came and fixed him food to take with him.

Johnnie Patton was cooking for us at the time and he helped me hide Billy the Kid as my husband had forbid me to feed Billy or harbor him in any way, as the Murphey Dolan faction had threatened to burn us out if we did, so I had to be very careful.

My oldest child, a boy, was about three years old, and Billy the Kid called him *Pardie*.

While Bob Olinger was guarding Billy the Kid he asked me to the hanging.

Billy said, "Mrs. Lesnett, if I am not there they can't hang me can they."

I was in Silver City about the time the Lincoln County War started, and stopped at Mrs. Antram's boarding house, and she told me about her young son getting into trouble and leaving home, but at that time I did not know that her son was Billy the Kid.[11]

Billy the Kid was a nice looking boy, about five feet seven inches tall, fair complected with blue grey eyes, and very small hands and feet. He wore nice looking clothes, a big cowboy hat and always had a red silk handkerchief tied around his neck. He was always so nice and considerate of women and children.

I never heard of Billy having a sweetheart in this part of the country. Billy the Kid's mother did not tell me the reason for his leaving home the first time I met her. A few years later I returned to Hudson Hot Springs and I went to see Mrs. Antrim, Billy's mother. She told me then that the reason her son had to leave home was because he had killed a man for making insulting remarks about her. He left home that night and she never saw nor heard from him again.

I never knew Bob Olinger very well. I just saw him the one time while he was guarding Billy the Kid. He was a big burly fellow, and every one that I ever heard speak of him said he was mean and over-bearing, and I know that he tantalized Billy while guarding him, for he invited me to the hanging just a few days before he was killed. Even after he was killed I never heard any one say a single nice thing about him.[12]

THE ARIZONA DAYS

CALLING HIMSELF KID ANTRIM, Billy worked as a cowboy in Arizona until forced to flee a murder conviction. After a card game at Bonito on August 17, 1877, Billy quarreled with Frank P. Cahill, a civilian blacksmith at nearby Camp Grant, and killed him. He escaped from the post guardhouse and returned to New Mexico. [12]

JIM BLAIR OF SANTA RITA

COLLECTED BY FRANCES E. TOTTY, 1937

Billie the Kid never did kill anyone in Silver City that story is all false. The story of him killing a man over Ed. Moulton is positively not true. Mr. Moulton never would read an article about Billie because he would get angry for he said, "They write so many lies about the boy, and I know the ones are false about his killings in Grant Co." Mr. Moulton's friendship for the family sprang from the day he began to stay in Mrs. Antrim's boarding house when he came to town.

When Billie left Grant Co. it was for a minor crime. Billie went to Arizona where he shot a blacksmith, the fellow was always teasing the boy, and Billie having a quick temper one day shot the fellow and left Arizona.

He came to Ed Moulton's sawmill on a half-starved horse and asked to stay awhile. Billie told Ed the trouble he had gotten into. Ed advised him not to stay too long around his place if he was running from the law.

Ed always had a good supply of food for his horses at the mill, when the boy had fed his horse until he gained some strength he told Ed that he was thinking about drifting over to Lincoln Co. and joining the war. Ed asked him which side he was going to join, and the boy didn't know. The boy left and never returned to the county.[13]

OTHO ALLEN OF DEMING

COLLECTED BY FRANCES E. TOTTY, 1938

My father, J. W. Allen, and mother came to Deming in 1882 a year before I was born. There wasn't a doctor in Deming at the time my people came to town. Dr. Stoval came to Deming in 1884 just before I was born.

He was just a lad and my mother would not have him as a doctor, because she said he hadn't had any experience, and she would rather have an older woman take care of her. Dr. Stoval is practicing over on the Mimbres River at the present time.

In 1884 my father moved to Whitewater, where two regiments of soldiers were stationed. He didn't have a job or any money and killed antelopes for the soldiers. He later bought a tent and started a saloon where he made enough money to get a start.

He moved to White Signal in 1885 and took squatters rights on a piece of land. Our first livestock was hogs and we slowly acquired a few cattle. My father was very conservative and was trying to get ahead. He saved a few $20 gold pieces, which I found and dropped through a crack in the floor. The story got out about me pushing the gold pieces through the floor and people got the impression that my father was rich and hoarding gold.

One night a knock was heard at the door. When we called "who is it?" the answer was "It's me." My father was away from home and mother wouldn't open the door. The man tried to get in the house and hung around for a couple of hours and finally went away. The next morning we found two large rocks and a heavy green club by the door. After that my father was very careful about his money.

Ceasar Brock killed the last mountain sheep in the Burro Mountains. I was a youngster at the time and could only reach half way around his horn with both hands.

The first time I saw Mr. Brock I was riding behind my father to camp. Father said, "Son, here comes some one with a large gun." It was in winter and was very cold. Father asked Mr. Brock to return to camp with us, which he did. He had been to our camp, but left as we didn't return to camp early. Mr. Brock said, I killed a deer up here and you can have it if you will go get it as it is too far for me to carry to my camp. The next morning we went with Mr. Brock to where the deer was and a wildcat had been there. Mr. Brock remarked that he just as well have his skin as anyone else, and left. That afternoon father and I was cleaning out a slue when one of us happened to look up and saw Mr. Brock standing on one of the highest peaks with the skin tied around his waist. Mr. Brock came off the side of that cliff as fleet as a deer.

Mr. Brock was raised around the Indians and to many is very queer. One never knew when to expect him at their elbow laughing, because he scared them. At dawn he might be at your camp some five or ten miles from his camp, and at dusk thirty miles away, and he was always afoot.

He had a gun that is marked T? S.V. which is generally believed to belong to the Adams party. The Gold Gulch country must be where the Adams Diggings are located for Mr. Brock found the gun in a cave in the Gulch. The land markings suit the Adams description. The mountain that resembles a woman's breasts can be seen. I have found several 45-70 Rim Fire shells in the Gulch, and several cradles that were made with pegs for nails. Mr. Brock used to come in with some nice nuggets and told us that he thought the Gulch was where the Adams Diggings were. He later showed us the gun that he had found with the initials carved on it.

There is a hole in the Gulch formed by water falling from a cliff in rainy weather. In this hole one can see a heart with an arrow through it, and turkey tracks in the rocks. How the Indians got in the hole to carve signs is a miracle to me. The sides of the hole are slick and curve slightly. There are many cliff dwellings around the Gulch, and Pit dwellings are found all along the range of mountains.

John Cummings told me the first time he saw Billie the Kid

14

was in Cochise. The Kid came into town and went to a saloon and said he was hunting work. The boy saw some men gambling and was soon in the game he was a stranger in the country, and as he seemed to have all of the luck and was taking all of the money, one of the men made a nasty remark. The Kid drew his gun and killed two of the men around the table and injured another. He walked out of the saloon as he had just been in the place for a drink, and walked over to his horse as unconcerned, looked back, and then jumped on and rode away. The men at the saloon had thought of him as a mere lad and were taken back when they found him quick on the draw. The boy left Cochise and was never seen there again.

In 1905 John MacMullen brought the first two cylinder car to Silver City. We all knew that a car would never go to Mogollon. Everyone thought Mr. MacMullen was rich as he had a car. We had always gone horseback and thought horse would be the only success-ful way of travel. We rode horses for fifteen cents apiece or two for twenty-five. One night Mr. Brock came to camp and asked me to ride one of his horses, I replied, "Mr Brock we are charging to ride horses now."

"How much?" Mr. Brock asked.

"Fifteen cents for one horse."

"I'd pay fifteen cents to see anyone ride my horse for he has throwed more than one."

"All right bring him over any time you have him up and I'll ride him."

Mr. Brock left and about nine that night he came to camp leading a large black horse. He said, "Let's see you ride him." I got my fifteen cents. Took off his Montgomery saddle with one stirrup shorter than the other, and put my saddle on the horse. The boys that were in bed and hadn't gotten up while I was saddling the horse got up when I got on him. That horse jumped through one of the tents and the chuck wagon. We rode through the camp and tore up things in general. In the early days when you rode a wild horse he was wild, but it was all in the game for we needed the money. We never minded a few hard falls, we expected them. We didn't mind sleeping but we had our old cowboy songs to sing and square dances to pass the time so life wasn't dull. [15]

15

►3◄

THE KILLING OF
SHERIFF WILLIAM BRADY

MAJOR WILLIAM BRADY BECAME THE SHERIFF of Lincoln County when it was first organized in 1869 and again in 1876, when he pledged loyalty to James J. Dolan. On February 18, 1878, Dolan's rival, John H. Tunstall, was ambushed and killed. Billy Bonney, who was arrested by Brady on February 20, joined several former Tunstall employees like himself and others in a vigilante group known as the Regulators to arrest Tunstall's killers. Six Regulators, including Bonney, spent the night of March 31, 1878, in Tunstall's Lincoln store and on the morning of April 1 ambushed Brady and four companions as they walked from Dolan's store to the courthouse. The Kid was wounded in the left thigh when he rushed into the street to retrieve his rifle, which Brady had impounded in the February arrest, from the fallen sheriff.[16]

ROBERT BRADY OF HONDO

COLLECTED BY EDITH L. CRAWFORD, 1937

My father, Major William Brady, was fifty-six years old when he was killed by Billy the Kid and his gang in Lincoln, New Mexico, April 1, 1878. Father, Billy Mathews, his chief deputy, George Heinman, George Peppin and Jack Long were on their way to the court house to open a term of court. Father and George Heinman had stopped to tell Timeoteo Analla, Ignacio Torres and Navor Chavez, they were members of the grand jury, that he was going to open court and adjourn it as he had a letter from the Judge saying he was afraid to come to Lincoln and hold court at that time. Billy

Mathews, Jack Long and George Peppin had walked on down the road ahead of them. After talking to the three jurors a few minutes, Father and Heinman started on down to the court house, which was later used as the Catholic Church. Just as they arrived in front of where the Penfield home now stands, Billy the Kid and his gang opened fire on them. Father fell mortally wounded; he was shot sixteen times in the back. George Heinman ran for his life and escaped without a scratch. Billy Mathews, Jack Long and George Peppin were in front of Mrs. Lupe Sisneros' house and they ran in there and watched the shooting from a window. Father's body lay in the street for an hour after he was killed and while he was laying there Billy the Kid and gang went out to where his body lay and were going to take his guns, when Billy Mathews saw them from the home of Mrs. Sisneros. He opened fire on them and ran away. Billy the Kid and his gang were firing on father from a high adobe wall which was built around the old tower which is now El Torreon. Everybody was afraid to go near father's body for quite awhile. Mrs. Saturnino Baca finally went out to where he lay and in a few minutes more people came out. They got a hack and took his body to the court house and later to our home, which was six and one half miles below Lincoln on the Rio Bonito. Father was buried on the flat out in front of our house where his body still rests.

My father was sheriff at the time the papers were issued to attach the McSween and Tunstall cattle. He sent Billy Mathews, his chief deputy, to get the cattle and bring them in to Lincoln. On the way back some of the Murphy-Dolan gang shot Tunstall, and the Lincoln County War was on.

When father heard of the killing of Tunstall he sent another deputy, Pablo Pino, to help bring the cattle in to Lincoln. They did not keep the cattle very long as Billy the Kid and his gang recovered the cattle and drove them back to the Pajarito Mountains and turned them loose. Most of them were stolen during the Lincoln County War. Billy the Kid and his gang were hiding in the mountains, just back of the McSween home in Lincoln and while there they sent a note to Vincente Romero to meet them in the Chaves flat, which is about three quarters of a mile southeast of Hondo, New Mexico. It was planned so that the Murphy-Dolan gang would

Interior of the Tunstall Store, Lincoln, New Mexico, ca. 1954. Photo courtesy Museum of New Mexico, Neg. No. 57241.

get hold of this information. The Murphy-Dolan gang immediately planned to way lay Billy the Kid and his gang on the Chaves flats. Billy and his gang were watching from their hiding place in the mountains and when they saw the Murphy-Dolan gang leave Lincoln they came into town and took possession of it. As soon as the Murphy-Dolan gang realized this was a trap they rushed back to Lincoln to find Billy and his gang in possession of the town. The town people were very much frightened for they knew there would be a battle between the two factions.

Billy the Kid's gang finally made a stand in the McSween home. The Murphy-Dolan gang surrounded the house. The town people were so alarmed that they sent for the soldiers from Fort Stanton, New Mexico, to come down and make peace between the two factions but their presence did no good. The Murphy-Dolan faction made plans to set the McSween house on fire. They sent a negro man by the name of George Dixon out to get all the coal oil he could find. When he returned with the oil they had some boxes piled up against the porch and they poured the oil on them and struck a match to them but Billy the Kid's gang were watching them and had some wet blankets that they threw on the fire and put it out. The Murphy-Dolan gang got some red shirts and soaked them in the coal oil, set them on fire and threw them at the house. Finally they got a spot to burning where the people in the McSween house could not get to it. The house began to burn and the smoke was so thick that they could not see on the outside so Bob Beckwith slipped up to the front porch and when McSween opened the door and started out Beckwith shot him dead in his tracks, and shot several others at the front door.

While this was going on at the front door of the house, Higinio Salazar started out the back door on the run, as he reached the yard he was hit by three bullets in the left shoulder and fell to the ground and made out like he was dead. Several of the Murphy-Dolan gang went up to him and wanted to shoot him between the eyes but a man by the name of John Kinney said, "No he is dead and his face looks pretty good so leave him alone," so they did, but on leaving several of the men picked up some old adobes that were in the yard and threw them on his body. He survived all of this and lived to be a very old man.

I remember one night Billy the Kid and his gang came to Lincoln and let all the prisoners out of jail. Jess Evans, Frank Baker, Tom Hale, Tom O'Fallard, Catrino Romero and Lucas Gallegos were the prisoners. The jail was a dugout, twenty-four by twenty-eight feet and about ten feet deep, on top of the ground were logs chinked up with mud, with a dirt roof and one door. They had a ladder that they put down in this dugout to put the prisoners in jail and when they were all inside they pulled the ladder up and hid it. When Billy and his gang came to town and found some of their pals in jail they hunted up the jailer (I don't remember his name), got the key and ladder and let all the prisoners out.

Another time Charlie Crawford, Marion Turner and Lucio Montoya were hid in the mountains just back of the Ellis house and started shooting at the Ellis house and barn. They shot Ben Ellis through the neck and killed two horses and one mule in the barn. When Billy's gang went after them and began shooting at them Lucio Montoya took to a corn patch and ran into Mrs. Lupe Sisneros' house and she hid him in a flour barrel. When the Kid's gang went up to her house and asked her if Montoya was there she replied that she had not seen him. After dark he got out of the flour barrel and made his get away.

A fellow by the name of Frank Freeman went into Sam Wortley's hotel in Lincoln. There were two negro soldiers sitting at the table. Freeman walked over to them and ordered them to get out. They told him they were waiting for their supper, that they had ordered it and they intended to pay for it and did not see why they couldn't stay and eat. Freeman pulled his six shooter and killed them both where they sat. He got on his horse, rode six and one half miles to our house below Lincoln. Father saw him coming and stepped outside the door. When Freeman came up he had two boxes of cartridges in his hand, he asked father for his cartridge belt. Father handed it to him and he filled it full of cartridges and turned to leave. He said to father as he was leaving, "You will be looking for me tomorrow, I just killed two negro soldiers in Sam Wortley's hotel in Lincoln." He got on his horse and rode away. Ten days later father captured him and turned him over to the officers at Fort Stanton, New Mexico.

Father worked for Murphy and Dolan when they had cattle and owned most of the Carrizozo flats. That was before he was sheriff and before the Lincoln County War.

I had many fights after the Lincoln County War. I used to fight with Higinio Salazar every time we met because he was one of Billy the Kid's gang. I always had a hatred of them because they killed my father. My father was born in Covan, Ireland, in 1825.[17]

GORGONIO WILSON OF ROSWELL

COLLECTED BY EDITH L. CRAWFORD, 1938

The day Billy the Kid, Frank McNab, Tom O'Fallered and others shot and killed Sheriff William Brady, my sister Junita and I

20

were playing in our front yard, when we heard shooting and looked up to see William Brady fall to a sitting position. He said, "Oh Lord" and tried to get up, but there was another round of shots and he fell back mortally wounded. This battle was fought in front of our house, in Lincoln, New Mexico.

Sheriff William Brady, Billy Mathews, Johnnie Hurley and Florencio Chavez were taking a prisoner down to the justice of the peace for trial, when the shooting started the prisoner ran for his life, jumped over an adobe wall and escaped. Billy the Kid and one of his pals started over to where Brady's body was laying in the street to get his guns. Billy Mathews and Johnnie Hurley were hid in the home of Mrs. Lupe Sisneros, watching through the window. When they saw Billy the Kid and his pal going toward Brady's body they shot at them and hit Billy the Kid in the leg. Billy and his pal ran back to their hide out which was an adobe corral just back of where the Penfield home now stands. My father, Green Wilson was hoeing onions just across the road from where the battle took place and he was shot in both legs between the hips and knees, just through the fleshy part of his thighs. He got away from the scene just as soon as he could and walked down to Isaac Ellis's home for medical care.

One time when my father Green Wilson was Justice of the Peace he gave Pat Garrett, then sheriff, a warrant to go to Seven Rivers and arrest Billy the Kid which he did and brought him into my father's office and said, "Judge, here is your man, what are you going to do with him," Pat said with a smile, "shoot him or turn him loose?" Billy still had on his guns.

At one time Billy the Kid and Pat Garrett were very good friends.[18]

MRS. J. P. CHURCH OF ROSWELL

COLLECTED BY GEORGIA B. REDFIELD, 1937

Major Brady received word from Judge Bristol that he would not try to hold the regular term of court in April at Lincoln as someone had told him that he was likely to be shot as Billy the Kid had started a frame-up with his gang to kill him.

Major Brady (who was sheriff of Lincoln County at the time) was on his way to open court and to make the announcement that Judge Bristol would not be there and to adjourn the court. The court house was in the center of town just east of where the Catholic Church is now. There have been different stories written of this location of the court house and of the shooting of Brady that were not true. I lived there in Lincoln at the time and know the locations and saw Brady after he was shot.

Green Wilson the Justice of the Peace lived just west of the court house. Gorgonio Wilson was a young boy at the time.

Later after the killing of Major Brady, Green Wilson moved just east of the court house and that was where Governor Wallace met Billy the Kid to offer clemency if he would give himself up to justice. That old adobe house is still there.

Brady was made a major during the Mexican War. He came with the California Column.

Major Brady (sheriff) had deputy sheriff George Hindman and Clerk of Court Billy Mathews with him when he was killed. He was on his way to adjourn court until more peaceful times. There was also a third man with them. I don't know who he was.

Billy the Kid and his gang were lying in wait for Major Brady, concealed by a wall near Green Wilson's place and while Major Brady was talking of having to adjourn court on account of the little "cow-thief," Billy the Kid who was getting more daring every day, he was fired on by the Kid and his gang. Major Brady was killed instantly. George Hindman fell. Ike Stockton who was near heard the shooting, he looked and saw Hindman moving his hand and ran to him. There was a "presa" (ditch) near; Ike Stockton gave Hindman a drink. He died in a few minutes. I saw Major Brady and Hindman when he fell. The bodies were taken away by men who were appointed to act as coroner's jury. Billy Mathews ran to a nearby house where Lupe Cisneros lived and began firing at Billy the Kid, who escaped with the rest of the gang of McSween men while Mathews were still shooting at him.

About Ollinger's and Bell's shooting, I know about that too. Billy the Kid himself told Goss the cook to saddle the horse which was feeding on the alfalfa field adjoining the court house. The cook helped to get the shackles off Billy the Kid's hands (I don't know how it was done) but he couldn't get them off his legs. An interesting feature of the shackles was that they were very crude handmade, and were not locked. They were welded on, and the Kid had to ride a mile and a half west of Lincoln before they were removed by a Mexican man who afterwards gave them to George Titsworth (now of Capitan) who has an interesting collection of relics at that place.[19]

►4◄

THE BATTLE OF BLAZER'S MILL

ON APRIL 4, 1878, SOME OF THE REGULATORS, including leader Dick Brewer and Billy Bonney, stopped at Blazer's Mill. Andrew J. (Buckshot) Roberts, a Dolan supporter, approached them there. In the ensuing shoot out Bonney, John Middleton, and George Coe were wounded. Both Roberts and Brewer were killed.[20]

A. N. BLAZER OF MESCALERO
AND LUCIUS DILLS OF ROSWELL

COLLECTED BY GEORGIA B. REDFIELD, 1937

Blazer's Mill, in Otero County on the Mescalero Apache Indian Reservation, is eighty-nine miles west of Roswell over U.S. Highway 380 and 70. Located in a green valley on the upper Tularosa Creek.

A sawmill was first built on the mill site before the Mexican War, and, it is thought, before settlement of the Rio Grande Valley by the Spanish people.

The buildings were torn down a number of times and rebuilt by different parties. It was not known as "Blazer's Mill" until about 1870. It was used as a sawmill until 1882 when the grist mill was built.

Dr. Joseph Hoy Blazer (born in Pennsylvania in 1828) built the first grist mill in 1882. Some of the members of the Blazer family who live on the old mill site at the present time are a son, grandson and great-grandson of Dr. Blazer.

A. N. Blazer, the son, was born in Iowa in 1865 before Dr. Blazer moved his family to New Mexico. As a small boy he was a favorite of the Indians. He was taken by them, the only white person, on Indian hunting expeditions. The Blazer family has always been interested in mechanics. He has done research and valuable development work on pumps, water wheels and engines.

Billy the Kid and his outlaw gang, in 1878, made this peaceful beauty spot around the mill the scene of a bloody gun-battle, in which "Buckshot" Bill Roberts and outlaw Dick Brewer were killed and others of the gang seriously wounded.

Twelve outlaws, including Billy the Kid, but led by Dick Brewer (the Captain of the gang at the time), gathered at the George Coe Ranch. With George Coe joining the bunch they started (as they claimed) after horse thieves. They ended their proposed jaunt at Blazer's Mill, arriving just before noon. They were cordially greeted by Dr. Blazer who knew two men of the bunch, Frank and George Coe.

Dr. Blazer asked the bunch to stay for dinner, warning them to keep a look-out for "Buckshot" Roberts, who was after them, as were also the soldiers stationed a mile away on the Indian Reservation.

A hundred dollar reward had been offered for each of the gang, dead or alive, who had been with the slayers when Sheriff Brady was slain.

Buckshot Roberts (so called because of his bravery under fire) had been a Texas Ranger and an Indian fighter. He, at this time, lived quietly on a little place on the Ruidoso. He offered himself for the dangerous job of bringing in the murderers and was accepted by the officials of the law at Lincoln. He had taken no active part before this in the feuds and war waged around him. While he had not witnessed the killing of Brady, he was determined to avenge his murder.

George Coe and John Middleton were stationed as guards to watch for Roberts, while the other men were eating dinner inside the Blazer home.

In a short while Roberts rode up as expected. As the guards watched alertly he dismounted from his mule and seeing he had placed himself at a disadvantage, he lowered his gun, resting it on his boot, and stood quietly. Recognizing some of the men who had come out from their dinner, he asked to speak with Frank Coe whom he had considered a friend and at whose home he had spent the night before and who knew Robert's plans for capturing the gang.

Frank Coe promised Roberts that if he would give himself up to the gang he would not be harmed. Roberts replied, "I will give myself up to no gang like Billy the Kid's, they are murderers and I will fight to the last ditch before I surrender to them."

Dick Brewer asked for volunteers to go around the house and take Roberts.

Charlie Bowdre, George Coe and Billy the Kid offered to go. Others said if they were killed they would try their hand.

Bowdre took the lead, George Coe and Billy the Kid were close behind. As soon as Bowdre turned the corner of the house he threw his gun on Roberts commanding him to throw up his hands.

"Not much Mary Ann," was Robert's reply. Both his and Bowdre's guns were fired simultaneously. Robert's bullet glanced off Bowdre's cartridge belt, struck and shattered George Coe's right hand, severing the trigger finger. Bowdre's ball went through Robert's stomach.

Roberts, mortally wounded, drove his enemies to cover, and fell back into the room. He dragged a feather bed to the door, rolled upon it and resumed his firing. Dick Brewer, concealed behind a log at the old saw mill, fired at the spot where he could dimly see the feather bed, not hitting Roberts; he raised his head to look and take another aim when Roberts shot him between the eyes, killing him instantly.

The outlaws swore revenge. Dr. Blazer quietly suggested that he would go around and see how badly Roberts was injured. He called out, "Roberts, I am Dr. Blazer, may I come in and help you?" Roberts gasped a reply, "No one can help me, I'm killed. It is all over."

Dr. Blazer entered, saw nothing could be done, and told the men there was no use fighting longer, Roberts would not live an hour.

The soldiers from the Indian Agency appeared in sight. The outlaws ran to the mountains and hid in the timber.

Roberts, brave to the last, died within four hours after he was shot.

The brave man, Roberts, who desired peace at any price, and his foe, an outlaw on whose head a price had been set, lay dead. Both victims of the feuds, passion for revenge, and the lust for killing, which spread through that part of New Mexico after the coming of Billy the Kid.

Both men lie buried on the Blazer Mill site. The two graves are the only evidence remaining of the fierce battle that took place on that now peaceful spot, nearly sixty years ago. [21]

►5◄

THE KILLING OF FRANK McNAB

*MARION TURNER AND JOHN JONES'S SEVEN RIVERS gang,
organized into a posse and on its way to Lincoln to help
Dolan, killed Frank McNab, wounded Ab Sanders, and
captured Frank Coe on April 28, 1878.* [22]

DONICINO MOLINA OF TULAROSA

COLLECTED BY EDITH L. CRAWFORD, N.D.

I was born in Belen, New Mexico, but have spent most of my life in Lincoln County.

I was living with my brother Jose Molina at Hondo, New Mexico, about two miles below the Fritz Ranch at the time of the Lincoln County War.

I happened to be near the Fritz spring when several of the Murphy men rode up to the spring—there were several of the McSween men there and both sides started shooting. A fellow by the name of Frank McNab was killed, and they shot Frank Coe's horse from under him, as he was running toward the river.

I often wonder how he escaped without a scratch, as there was so many shots fired at him. He was captured and taken to Lincoln.

I knew Billy the Kid well as he stopped at my brother's house many times. [23]

►6◄

THE McSWEENS' LINCOLN HOME BURNS

ALEXANDER A. AND SUSAN McSWEEN'S LINCOLN house was burned on the night of July 19, 1878, the culmination of a five-day battle which began on July 15. The Kid, Tom O'Folliard, and Jim French manged to escape the shooting, but others, including McSween himself, were killed in the fusillade. After igniting the house and McSween's body, Dolan supporters rampaged through Lincoln.[24]

FRANCISCO GOMEZ OF LINCOLN

COLLECTED BY EDITH L. CRAWFORD, 1937

I was fourteen years old at the time of the Lincoln County War. I was irrigating a piece of land just back of the McSween home across the Bonita River. I remember seeing several men coming up the river from the east side of town—then I saw the Fort Stanton soldiers marching up the road towards the home of my compadre, Liso Salas—then I noticed that they were coming down the road and they stopped in front of the McSween home.

The officer was talking to some in the house, at the same time the men I saw coming up the river had gone up to the wall back of the house. The next thing I saw, the house was on fire; and I ran from the place I was working and hid—because there was a lot of shooting going on.

I remember well seeing some one carrying a person across the river after the shooting stopped. Later on I learned that it was Igenio Salazar, who was wounded that day as he ran from the

29

McSween home.

I was so scared I couldn't tell just what all was taking place. I knew Billy the Kid well.[25]

COLLECTED BY EDITH L. CRAWFORD, 1937

In 1877 I worked in the home of Mr. McSween in whose house Billy the Kid took up abode at that time. There we both stayed, I as a worker and he as a boarder. We stayed some 7 or 8 months and I knew this young man to be kind and gentlemanlike with me and with all the inhabitants of Lincoln. During the time he was there I left this home but he remained; a little while later I saw him leave here with some other people from here on a search for some Texan assailants who were molesting the people by shooting in the streets. The sheriff gathered some people together with Billy the Kid for the search. The assailants were above the Ruidoso River at a place called "La Cuesta." There they fought and one was killed and two taken prisoner. From then on I did not see him again until in 1881 when I saw him in jail. I do not know where he was arrested. He remained there up to the time that he killed the two guards.

I have heard from several people who were around close at the time that he killed the guards, that they took him from the jail to a room above the court room and this is where he killed the first guard, and he killed the other outside the house on the side of the Calle Carmen; this I know through information from neighbors who saw the killings. I did not see him at the time. This is all I know relative to Billy the Kid.[26]

MANUEL AGUILAR OF CAPITAN

COLLECTED BY EDITH L. CRAWFORD, 1937

I was born at Manzano, New Mexico. My people moved to Lincoln County when I was one year old.

In the year of 1878 we lived on the north side of the Bonito

River, about one and one-half miles west of the town of Lincoln, close to the graveyard.

I was about ten years old at that time and remember well when my compadre, Teodoro Farmer and myself were playing near the graveyard and the first thing we knew some one was pointing a gun at us; and believe me, we started running, very much scared.

We saw the man was laughing and at the same time he told us to stop, that he was not going to hurt us, and we asked him who he was; and he replied, "I am Billy the Kid." I know it was the Kid for I saw him several times later on as he visited the home of Jim Farmer, who lived near us.

At that time I remember well the day the McSween house burned. I was close to the road when the Fort Stanton soldiers went marching by toward Lincoln; and later in that day we could see the smoke from the burning building. Later on we were told that the Murphy gang had burnt the McSween house, killed Mr. McSween and wounded Iginio Salazar—and that Billy the Kid had escaped from the building unhurt.[27]

MRS. LORENCITA MIRANDA OF LINCOLN

COLLECTED BY EDITH L. CRAWFORD, 1939

I was born August 10, 1861, in the town of Las Placitas, New Mexico, in Socorro County, New Mexico. (Las Placitas is now the town of Lincoln and is in Lincoln County, New Mexico.) My father Gregorio Herrera married my mother Gerelda Torres in Manzano, New Mexico, about the year 1860. They moved to Las Placitas, New Mexico, and I was born there. On August 18th, 1861, about ten days after I was born, my father was killed in a drunken row in Las Placitas. Another man was killed at the same time and we never were sure who did kill my father. After Father's death my mother went back to Manzano to live with her people. My mother gave me to one of my aunts, Trinidad Herrera (who was nick-named Chinita) who, with my mother moved back to Las Placitas when I was about two years old. I have lived the rest of my life in Lincoln

County. I will soon be 78 years old.

In the year 1869, when I was eight years old, all of the territory lying east of the Mal Pais was created into Lincoln County, and the county seat was established at Las Placitas and the name was changed to Lincoln.

I was married to Jose Delores Miranda in January 1877. We were married in the Catholic Church at the Torres Ranch, by Father Sambrano Tafoya of Manzano, New Mexico. This church is about six miles west of Lincoln, New Mexico. I remember that we had to walk about five miles to the church to get married.

My husband had a two roomed adobe house built for us to live in. It had a dirt floor. We had no stove and I had to cook on the fireplace. All eight of my children were born in Lincoln. Seven of them are dead and buried there. My youngest son, Emelio Miranda, is married and has twelve children. He lives in Lincoln and is the post-master there. One of my grandsons lives with me on my little farm, a half mile west of the town of Lincoln. I raise a few chickens and a small garden which helps to keep me busy.

The house where I was born in Las Placitas (now Lincoln) stood on the site of the old Laws Sanitarium. The place then belonged to Sabino Gonzales, who was one of the men that helped build the old Torreon in 1855. My father-in-law Felipe Miranda also helped to build the Torreon. This old Torreon was rebuilt and dedicated in 1935, by the Chaves County Archaeological and Historical Society.

My husband and I were living on our farm just above Lincoln, New Mexico, all during the Lincoln County War. We liked both factions so we never took any part in the war. I remember the day the McSween home was burned. We could see the flames and smoke from our house but we stayed at home for we were scared to death to stick our heads out of the house. We could also hear some of the shooting. Billy the Kid came to our house several times and drank coffee with us. We liked him for he was always nice to the Spanish people and they all liked him.

My aunt, Chinita Herrera, started to walk to Socorro, New Mexico, to see her brother. (I do not remember the year.) She was seen on the road to Socorro by Mrs. Susan McSween Barber who

Susan McSween Barber. Photo courtesy Museum of New Mexico, Neg. No. 50345.

gave her a drink of water and some food. She was not far from a ranch house and Mrs. Barber thought she would get along all right, but my aunt was never seen or heard of again. We never did know what became of her.

My mother married a man by the name of Octaviano Salas and lived in Lincoln, New Mexico, until her death in September 1926.

My husband Jose Delores Miranda died October 28, 1928, in Lincoln and was buried here.[28]

CLARA FRESQUEZ OF LINCOLN

COLLECTED BY LESTER B. RAINES, 1936

Last summer the clerk who works in Mr. Penfield's store in Lincoln, New Mexico, near our home was cleaning the basement, where there had accumulated a pile of old papers, magazines, books and letters from the time when Lincoln was the county seat and when it was the center of the Lincoln County War.

John Luna, the clerk, found a very old letter, yellow, crumpled, and still unopened. His curiosity aroused, he picked it up, opened it, and read:

"Dear MacSwain,
    Behind the door near the basement are a thousand dollars—get them.
    Your friend,
    Billy."

In those days MacSwain was the owner of the store and Billy the Kid made frequent stops there. Next to the store was MacSwain's home, set afire in the famous gun battle in which MacSwain lost his life.

The house, however, was rebuilt and finally came into possession of the Fresquez family. After search of the store for the buried money had failed, it occurred to my father and Luna to search MacSwain's old home, as the door there might have been the one Billy referred to.

Hence my father, Isidro Fresquez, looked behind all the doors and also looked for a basement, even though he had lived in the house for thirty years without knowing of any door leading down. He lifted up part of the floor and discovered that there was a basement. He kept looking until he found melted silver pieces and a few shards of pottery.

If this was Billy's treasure it was not the quantity of melted silver to be worth a thousand dollars. Whether we had found the spot he mentioned, whether the money had been earlier removed, or whether the few melted pieces were the remains of this or another hoard, we have never been able to decide.[29]

►7◄

THE KID PAYS A VISIT

THE LEGENDARY BILLY THE KID has been called "the American Robin Hood," an outlaw to the powerful and a courteous, congenial, and loyal friend to the powerless. He was also popularly thought to be a skilled musician, dancer, and lover.[30]

A. P. ANAYA OF VAUGHN

LETTER TO WILLIAM STEELE DEAN, 1926

Dear Mr. Dean: I accuse that I have in my hands a letter from you, dated July 29, 1926.

The same I had not answered because I received it at the time I was leaving for Las Vegas, and other parts of Pecos River. And I came back yesterday the 4th. of August. And today I have been seated to answer your letter. Sir, I believe that you have taken it with interest to know of the life and acts of Billy the Kid. I will tell you that what you have seen from what I have said of Billy, is not a fourth of what I know of Billy the Kid. I could give you the story of Billy since the first day I knew Billy, that was since the 14th of June 1878. From there on I was seeing him nearly every day, except when he went out some place for a few days, and then he returned back to Ft. Sumner. I know of everything he done while he was at Ft. Sumner. I know by himself since he left New York, when he arrived at Ft. Sumner how long he stayed there. It was in the year 1872 when he came to Ft. Sumner, their [sic] he worked with the father of Pete Maxwell until 1874. From there he went to Bosque Grande to a cattle ranch belonging to James Chisuim [sic] their he worked until war broke out at Murphey and McSweens. They worked with Mr. Chisuim to bring cattle they stole from the other

36

Morfes. And the ones they drove to Texas to Diablo River. Mr. Chisuim offered them $5 per head for all the cattle they would bring him, they brought him about 5000. The Morfes would take them and the Chisuims would bring them until war broke out. And when the guard of soldiers was put in favor of the Morfes, they killed Moquesuin and there Billy killed Roberto Beques at the house of Moquesuin. This was in June 1878 when Billy and his companions about 30 between Americans and Mexicans came to my sheep camp, about three miles west of Ft. Sumner. Since then he was living in Ft. Sumner until the 25th of December 1880. When they were taken by President [sic] Garrett, the 26th day of December. They took him to Las Vegas and from there to Santa Fe. There they held him for a long time looking for a way to indict him but they could not find cause. Then they took him to Las Cruces there they held him for a long time, they could not indict him and they brought him to Lincoln where they indicted him for a man that the people killed. Forty men were after Billy and his companions for a theft of some 80 head of cattle belonging to a man by the name of Sibs Grey, from Capitan. They killed this man in a mail route on the east of Gallina Mountains between Pinos Well and Whiterocks. For this man they indicted him and [he] was sentenced to be hanged on the 13th of September 1881, and on the 10th, three days before he killed the two guards, and came out on the 16th of September 1881. He came to my father's house at Sibolo 15 miles south of Ft. Sumner from there after staying 14 days at the house of my father, he went to Ft. Sumner there he stayed about 20 days and then he came back again to my father's house, there he stayed for two days until my father made him go to El Llano Estacado, (staked valley) to see if he could save his life for some time, but he left in an October day something like the 20th and it was very cloudy, and he said if I don't get lost and can go to Los Portales I go but if I can't I will come back. Accordingly he got lost and came to a place they call Tul where the band of sheep of Pete Maxwell were, there he remained with the shepherds until November 1881, he went to a ranch belonging to a man by the name of Tom Yerve of Las Vegas. There he spent the rest of that winter, until the 5th of May 1882, that he came to Ft. Sumner and there he stayed up to the 22nd of June that President Garrett killed him, and we buried him at the Military Cemetery on the 23rd.

This is in brief, if you want the history of what Billy the Kid done since the year 1872, that he came to Ft. Sumner of 12 years of age and died on the 22nd of June, 1882, 10 years he lived between Ft. Sumner, Roswell, and Lincoln, during this 10 years he killed 22 men, all Americans, except 5 Apaches that he killed 12 miles west of Roswell.

Now the complete history [of] what he done during this time is very long and I can not give it to you because I do not know if you read Spanish and I don't know how to write Inglish, I can talk and I can write a little but I haven't the satisfaction of being correct, if you can find the way that they translate it from Spanish, I can write you the history of Billy and give you an information of the life and acts of Billy. Where he stayed and by whom he was accompanied until the day of his death. I don't know if this is agreeable to you for writing you in Spanish but I can't do it in no other way, here we have nobody that can translate from Spanish, know the reason why I write you in my own language. I hope you write me and tell me what more you want of the history of Billy.

Very respectfully   A. P. Anaya[31]

MILNOR RUDOLPH

COLLECTED BY LESTER B. RAINES, 1936

The present Milnor Rudolph is grandson of Milnor Rudolph who was the foreman of the coroner's jury and signer of the inquest held over Billy the Kid. His uncle, Charles Rudolph, was in the posse with Pat Garrett when the notorious outlaw was captured near Fort Sumner. The stories here given were told Milnor Rudolph by his father and uncle.

Charles Rudolph was hoeing one day in the field when a young lad rode up and asked for something to eat. He immediately went to the house and brought out some food. The boy was most grateful.

"You were so good to give me something to eat. I'd like to do something for you. Your hat is old. Take mine; it's new." With that he exchanged hats and was off. Presently a band of men came up the road and Charles Rudolph barely escaped with his life. The posse were hunting Billy the Kid and, recognizing his hat on the boy working in the fields, surrounded him. After discovering their mistake the leader explained their purpose and Charles Rudolph joined the posse.

The elder Mr. Rudolph was postmaster of the little settlement of Sunnyside not far from Fort Sumner where many of Billy's escapades took place.

One day while Billy was at Fort Sumner a man pointed his gun at him and said, "Look out, Billy, I'm going to fire."

He did but the gun did not go off. Billy's did, and he and his gang cooly mounted their horses and rode off to Sunnyside where they went into the postoffice. The Kid had received a newspaper and sat down to read. One of the outlaws said to Mr. Rudolph, "Things are getting pretty warm at the fort."

"What's happened now?"

"A man was just killed," and he pointed to Billy.

"Why did you kill him Billy?"

"His gun wouldn't fire, and mine did."

Another time the gang went to rob a store. Some of them entered, others went above and let a man down head first through an opening in the ceiling. Those in the store immediately fired. In the confusion which followed, Billy and his companions had no difficulty in helping themselves.

Billy the Kid was very fond of milk. One day he came into Mr. Rudolph's home and asking for a glass of milk walked over to a pitcher on the table to help himself. Mrs. Rudolph was distressed, as the pitcher contained all the milk she could get that day for her baby. Still, she feared to refuse the outlaw.

"You can't have it, Billy. That's all there is and it's for the baby," said Mr. Rudolph, coming to his wife's rescue.

"But I'm the Kid and I want it," retorted the boy.

"You can't have it," persisted Mr. Rudolph.

Mrs. Rudolph gesticulated frantically to her husband, saying, "Let him have it, Milnor. I'll make some *atole* for the baby."

Billy saw her distress, put down the pitcher and walked from the room, remarking, "All right, Rudolph. I can eat other things and the baby can't."[32]

ISMAEL VALDEZ

COLLECTED BY LESTER B. RAINES, 1936

Grandmother was reared by Mr. Rudolph, an uncle, one of the characters often mentioned in history in connection with Billy the Kid. She lived in Fort Sumner in Lincoln County, where most of the events of Billy's life took place.

Grandmother says, "Billy at a very early age was one of the toughest *hombres* of the West. He had long curly hair; he was polite to women; he could play the piano well. The greatest delights Billy had were fighting, horseback riding, dancing, and playing the piano."

Billy often came to Fort Sumner and stopped at Mr. Rudolph's home for a night's lodging. He and his companions on entering handed their guns to Mr. Rudolph for safe keeping. Grandmother tells how Billy and his associates used to go to dances "packed with precious jewels": their guns.

One of the bloodiest occurrences in Billy's career was the blowing out of a store belonging to a Fort Sumner resident. Billy's crowd stopped at this big store for whiskey. The storekeeper refused to open his door to the unruly gang. The affront angering them, the crowd retreated to a safe distance and began shooting at barrels of powder which they spied through the store window. The powder exploded, the store went up in a rush of flame, the storekeeper lost his life, and one of Billy's crowd was mortally injured.[33]

BERTA BALLARD MANNING

COLLECTED BY GEORGIA B. REDFIELD, 1937

I was a child, age ten years, when we came from Fort Griffin, Texas, in 1879 with our parents, A. J. Ballard and Katherine

Redding Ballard and settled in Fort Sumner, New Mexico.

"The homes of all the families at the fort were built around the patio, and there was a set of drunken men who proceeded to shoot up the place, because the proprietor of the store refused to sell them more whiskey. A keg of powder was lit by a shot, exploded, and the store and our home were demolished.

"We then moved to Lincoln and were living there when 'Billy the kid' killed Ollinger and Bell and made his escape. However, I did not see the shooting. I don't see how my mother ever stood the excitement and anxiety of those wild lawless days. Of course we children didn't realize the danger of the outlaws shootings and escapades, that kept the old town of Lincoln in a constant turmoil.

"Yes, I remember Billy the Kid real well, he was not rough looking and was very quiet, unassuming and friendly. I never saw anything ugly about him or in his manners. I was a special child friend of Billie's, he took me on his lap and petted me when he came frequently to our home.

"He was kind and could be a good friend, but I am sure we should not make a hero of Billy, for after all he was a bandit and a killer.

"Billy was killed July 14, 1881, at Fort Sumner by Pat Garrett—in execution of his duty as sheriff—the following year after we moved to Lincoln. We had moved to Roswell when Billy was killed.

"Pat Garrett was a brave man, he knew it was Billie's life or his, for the boy would never have been taken alive. So to Pat Garrett we owe the accomplishment of freeing New Mexico of a dangerous outlaw and killer."[34]

JOSE MONTOYA OF JICARILLA

COLLECTED BY EDITH L. CRAWFORD, 1937

I knew Billy the Kid during the Lincoln County War. I was 11 years old at that time. Billy the Kid, Anastacio Martinez, a man by the name of Meleton (I never knew his last name), and a negro by the name of George Washington stole some horses from the

Indians and drove them over to my brother-in-law's ranch on the southeast side of the Capitan Mountains. This place was called Raton. Billy would let me ride his horse and also any of the Indian ponies that was gentle enough for me to ride. They stayed three or four days with us and I slept with Billy the Kid.

The government sent a bunch of soldiers from Fort Stanton to Lincoln to keep peace between the two factions there. Billy was in Lincoln at the time the soldiers came and he got a long stick and put a white handkerchief on the end of it and held it up and waved it and rode out of town accompanied by Anastacio Martinez, Meleton, and the negro man.

Billy was a small man with a small sharp nose, his two front teeth were large and stuck out in front. He was a nice fellow and well liked by the natives. He was awful good to the Mexican people and stayed with them most of the time and talked good Spanish. I saw Billy the Kid while he was in jail waiting to be hanged for the murder of Sheriff Brady.

I never heard of him having a sweetheart around this part of the country. I was living in Lincoln at the time Billy the Kid killed Bell and Ollinger and got away but I did not see him as every one was afraid to come out of their houses until he had left town.

I don't know what became of the rest of the men that were with Billy the Kid, except George Washington, the negro. He was married to a Mexican woman but he ran away with one of Captain Baca's daughters. This Captain Baca was well thought of in the community. The people of Lincoln caught this negro and killed him and then hanged his body up to a post in the yard of his wife. I never heard Billy the Kid speak of his mother.[35]

GUADALUPE BACA DE GALLEGOS OF LAS VEGAS

COLLECTED BY BRIGHT LYNN, 1938

For many years Mr. and Mrs. Gallegos ran a small store at San Ilario. Their store stood close to the main road, and almost every traveler who passed stopped in to buy something and to pass the time of day. One day Mrs. Gallegos returned to the store from a visit with one of her neighbors. Her husband was in front of the store, talking to an American cowboy in Spanish. When her husband saw her come in, he called to her and said, "Lupita, I want you to meet a friend of mine. This is Billy the Kid."

Mrs. Gallegos says that she has always been a brave woman, but when she found herself actually face to face with Billy the Kid she almost fainted. The Kid seemed to be in a talkative mood, for he started telling Mrs. Gallegos about his adventures, and for emphasis he drew his gun and shot a couple of holes in the ceiling. The neighbors all came running to find out what all the shooting was about, but upon finding it was Billy the Kid they all started running the other way.

The next time Mrs. Gallegos saw Billy the Kid she was in the store by herself. He came in, bought some things, and left. Mrs. Gallegos says that he was always very courteous and that he was, in her opinion, a real gentleman.

Mrs. Gallegos knew Sostenes, a member of Billy's gang, very well. His parents were good people and lived in Los Alamos. As far as she knew, Sostenes was always a good boy and it was hard for her to believe that he would turn outlaw. When he did turn, however, he turned with a vengeance. Mrs. Gallegos was acquainted with an old man who was half blind and he told her the following incident:

One day, while he was traveling on his burro, Billy the Kid and Sostenes rode up. Sostenes said, "Billy, let's kill this old blind man just to see how old blind men die."

"Let him alone," commanded Billy. "He's doing us no harm." The old man thought his day had come, and when Billy prevented Sostenes from killing him the Kid became the old man's hero.[36]

Dr. M. G. PADEN OF CARRIZOZO

COLLECTED BY EDITH L. CRAWFORD, 1937

I remember well the first time that I met Billy the Kid. It was in the year 1880 and several of my friends and I had gone to a Mex-

43

ican wedding celebration out in the mountains, and had camped just below the house where the celebration was to be held. Billy the Kid was at the house and of course he was very curious to find out who we were. He asked Dick Young, a friend of ours, who the crowd of white men were. When Dick told him that we were not officers and were friends of his, Billy came down to our camp. He wore a six shooter on his hip and carried a Winchester, and I could see that he was a little suspicious of us as his eyes missed nothing that went on. He was a young fellow, I should say about 19 or 20 years old, weighed about 135 pounds, light complected, with blue grey eyes and had very small hands and feet. His two front teeth were large and protruded. He was a nice and polite chap. One thing that struck me as very funny at the time was that he had on a black dress coat, his trouser legs stuffed in his boot tops and a large light hat. While standing talking to us he had his Winchester standing in front of him with both hands over the end of the barrel. He was manager of the celebration that night, and he asked every one that had on a gun to please take it off, as they wanted to have a nice peaceable dance. In those days every body carried a gun.

Bob Olinger was a bad hombre. Pat Garrett told me one time that he was so mean that he would be afraid to sleep with him.[37]

MR. SHUTZ, SON-IN-LAW OF MRS. CARLOTA BRENT OF SILVER CITY

COLLECTED BY WILLIAM STEELE DEAN, 1938

Mrs. Carlota Brent, 601 Cooper, Silver City, N.M. Mother-in-law of Mr. Shutz. From Mr. Shutz, almost verbatim:

Mr. Brent was a cattle inspector during the Lincoln County War. Once he and his deputy cornered Billy in a house. Billy called out that he would surrender if Mr. Brent would send his deputy in after him. This was done. In a few moments Billy came running from the house. Mr. Brent called to him to put his hands up, which he didn't do. So Mr. Brent shot at him and Billy fell to the ground. Mr. Brent, thinking Billy would not surrender without reaching for a gun, fired again. This time he knocked dirt all over Billy's face. Billy stumbled up and held up his hands. Mr. Brent rushed over and was surprised to find the man was his deputy and not Billy. Inside the house Billy had forced the deputy to change clothes with him. Billy had a horse that would come whenever he whistled to it and of course Billy had escaped out the back way.

Mrs. Brent says that almost everyone liked Billy so well they would gladly have offered to help him get away from the law or hidden him. She says he was handsome and did not have some of the features that some biographers attribute to him. She says she herself was smitten with him.

The position of cattle inspector was dangerous and it was almost impossible to identify hides as there would be sometimes over a half dozen brands on each hide. If the cattle inspector accused anyone, a half dozen would be equally guilty and all get to fighting him or among themselves and start a new range war.

Mr. Brent was a merchant at one time and once sent his wagons from "Silver" to the Mogollons with loads of flour. There was an Indian attack and, although the drivers escaped, the wagons were destroyed. All of the flour was dumped out into a large pile as the Indians wanted only the sacks. The mound of flour stayed there in the Mogollons a long time and it all made quite a story to be told around cow-camps and frontier towns.

When he first started the store Mr. Brent had a partner from the east who brought a cash register and a tall cabinet with many drawers in it to keep the money in. Mr. Brent said he didn't need this contraption. Everything he sold was paid for with a pinch of gold-dust; sometimes he would receive more dust than the article was worth and sometimes less, but it all averaged a very good profit. One morning he missed several thousand dollars. He thought someone had stolen it. For some reason he went out into the back-yard of the store to get a box. When he broke up the box he found the money which he had hidden there and forgot about doing so.

"Dry-gulching" (ambushing) was a popular method of disposing of your enemies or a knife thrown in the dark.

In the pioneer days most graves were lined with brick.[38]

►8◄

THE DEATHS OF TOM O'FOLLIARD AND CHARLES BOWDRE

ON DECEMBER 15, 1880, Governor Lew Wallace offered a $500 reward to whomever delivered Billy the Kid to Lincoln County sheriff Pat Garrett, who had been elected on November 2. On December 18, Garrett ambushed and killed the Kid's companion, Tom O'Folliard, at Fort Sumner. Another crony, Charles Bowdre, was killed on December 23 at Stinking Springs, where Billy Bonney and others were captured by Garrett's posse.[39]

BALLAD: CAMPAIGN OF THE "BILITOS"

CAMPAÑA DE LOS BILITOS

COLLECTED AND TRANSLATED
BY AURORA LUCERO WHITE,
1936

It was on the 17th of December
that Pat Garrett arrived
asking Puerto de Luna
that it think of giving aid
for it is at Fort Sumner
that the famous "Bilitos" are to be
found.

Quickly there is sent out a
messenger
in order to appoint
mounted and armed men
skillful in fighting.
By afternoon all were

Diez y siete de diciembre
Pat Garrett nos va llegando
pidiendo a Puerto de Luna
Su ayuda que vayan dando
que en Fort Sumner se hallan
los "Bilitos" mentados.

Pronto sale un mensajero
con presicion a nombrar
hombres montados y armados
y diestros para pelear.
Todos juntos en la tarde

ready to leave
but upon seeing Americans
some began to slip away.

All admitted defeat,
being a people disunited
why they were even ashamed
to go out in the campaign!
Only Juan Roybal went out
from that misadventured town
I shall not go into details
for it would be quite useless.

Also two strangers
although not natives of the place
left just a little behind
to place their lives in danger,
in order to put to shame
certain prominent individuals
who were wont to brag of their
        strength
considering themselves very brave.

Of those who feel the most injured
I ask—why did you not go
to apprehend the rascals
who so much damage caused?

And let no one feel injured
for that is not my intention
However, so much slander has
        been spread
that that is my sole motive.

We reached Fort Sumner
about day-break
and by three in the afternoon
we were covered with snow
There we obtained information
that there had already departed
the "Billys" the previous
        afternoon
headed for Ojo del Taiban.

estaban para salir
Porque velan Americanos
se empiezan a escabullir.

Toditos se derrotaron
pues es gente desunida
¿No darles una vergüenza
de salir a la partida?
Solo Juan Roybal salió
de esa plaza desgradiada
particulares no nombro
porque sería para nada.

También dos extranjeritos
sin ser del dicho lugar
salieron aunque atrasito
sus vidas a peligrar,
para que les diera vergüenza
a unos ciertos prominentes
que hablan mucho de sus fuerzas
teniéndose por valientes.

A los mas perjudicados
pregunto por que no fueron
a tomar a los malvados
que tanto mal les hicieron?

Ninguno quede agrabiado
pues no es esa mi intención;
mas, es tanto lo que han hablado
que es lo que me da razón.

Llegamos a Fort Sumner
cerca de la madrugada;
para las tres de la tarde
nos cubría una nevada
Allí nos dieron razón
que habían salido ya los "Biles"
la anterior tarde
para el "Ojo del Taibán."

The old hospital at the Fort
as a headquarters we designated,
a bad place for so many people,
but we found ample
    accommodations.
But we were unfortunate
to have Bob Campbell find out
about our arrival at the Fort,
there being some one to advise
    him.

Morning of the 19th
Johnny, the one from Brazil,
    arrived
and said that Bob Campbell
had already brought the message
that Pat Garrett with five men
was at the Fort since daybreak.
The "Biles" were about to set
    forth
but this discouraged them.

With reluctance Jose
was made by Pat to write a note
to "Bilito" that
Campbell he was to contradict
Upon receiving it, the "Billys"
to Bosque ventured forth.
Immediately they set out
and arrived nonchalantly.

At the home of Smith
supper had been prepared
but never did they expect
what we gave to them.
Carelessly we sat about playing in
our room
when the sentinel arrived
and gave us the notice.

We all arose
and went out to the Portal.

El viejo hospital del Fuerte
para cuartel designamos,
Mal lugar para tanta gente
mas bien, nos acomodamos.
Tuvimos la mala suerte
de que Bob Campbell supiera
de nuestra llegada al Fuerte
pues hubo quien le dijera.

Mañana del diez y nueve
Johnny, el de Brazil, llegó
y dijo que ya Bob Campbell
la noticia les mandó
que Pat Garrett con 5 hombres
en el Fuerte amaneció.
Ya iban a venir los "Biles"
y esto les desanimó.

Con repugnancia a José
le hizo Pat que le escribiera
al "Bilito" una notita
que al Campbell contradijera
Al recibirla los "Biles"
ir al Bosque se arriesgaron.
Luego tomaron su camión
y descuidados llegaron.

En casa de Smith
preparada tenían la cena, supimos,
pero nunca esperaban
la que nosotros les dimos.
Estábamos descuidados
en nuestro cuarto jugando
cuando llegó el sentinela
y el aviso nos va dando.

Toditos nos levantamos
y salimos al Portal.

Some went out the front,
and some went to the corral.
Tom Folliard was at the head
since he was the strongest.
He felt his body deaden
with a bit of lead.

We who went to the corral
scarcely turned the corner
when we saw a figure on horseback
even through the heavy mist.
We only struck the horse
because of his swiftness,
for he only carried his rider
to the spring of Taiban.

Stop! screamed Pat Garrett
the deputy marshall
when there arrive Tomas Folliard
to the edge of the gate.
Tomas in a second
took out his gun
but he scarcely had time
to take direct aim.

Pat Garrett took one shot at him
and the horses became frightened.
We knew he was wounded
by the scream he gave.
His horse dragged him
a short distance
where he went to lament
being in great pain.

He then urged his horse
since he could no longer see
whence the people had
    congregated.
He shouts that he is wounded
and begs to be left alone
for he had made up his mind
to give himself up.

Unos salen por adelante
y otros fuimos al corral.
Tom Folliard venia adelante
pues el era el más valiente.
Sintió su cuerpo pesado
con un plomito caliente.

Los que fuimos al corral
no mas volteamos la esquina
vimos un bulto a caballo
aunque había mucha noblina.
Solo al caballo le dimos
por su mucha liviandad,
pues no llevo a sus montador
mas que al ojo del Taibán.

¡Alto! les gritó Pat Garrett
el diputado mariscal
cuando llegó Tomás Folliard
a la orilla del portal.
El Tomás en un momento
a su pistola acudió
pero no tuvo más tiempo
y apenas la apuntó.

Pat Garrett le tiró un tiro
y el caballo se espantó.
Supimos que iba herido
por el grito que pagó
Su caballo sacó
a una corta distancia
a donde se fué a quejar
pues estaba con mucha ansia.

Ya dirijió su caballo
pues ya le faltaba su vista
hacia donde estaba la gente
toda preparada y lista
gritó que venía herido
y que ya no le tiraran
pues venía decidido
que su persona tomaran.

We then took the horse	Ya tomamos el caballo
by the halter we lead him	y de diestro lo llevamos
well sheathed in its holster his	bien montada le pistola
pistol we found.	en su cubierta la hallamos.
We took him inside	Lo metimos para adentro
for he no longer "put up a fight."	pues ya el defensa no hacia.
We stretched him on the floor	Lo tendimos en el suelo
because there were no beds.	porque allí camas no había.
His body was laid to rest	Su cuerpo fué sepultado
with not a little ceremony	con no muy poca ceremonia
and we all accompanied him	y todos lo acompañamos
no longer feeling irony.	pues se nos quito la ironiá.
The aforementioned shooting,	El tiroteo antedicho
to the gang of evil doers,	a la tropa de malvados
occurred at about eight	sucedió como a las ocho
and they left defeated.	y salieron derrotados.
Well, the rest of the comrades	Pues los demás compañeros
who Tomas had accompanied	que a Tomas acompañaban
were at the time of the shooting	iban cuando el tiroteo
on their way back, as if on wings.	para atras que alas les faltaban.
They headed toward Taiban	Al Taibán se dirijieron
with a horse that had been	con un caballo baleado
wounded	como dije antes que era
and as I said before	de Dave Rudabaugh, el mentado.
it had belonged to Dave	
Rudabaugh.	
On the night of the 22nd	El veinte y dos en la noche
we left Fort Sumner	del Fort Sumner salimos
with the cold very sharp	con un fríto muy crudo
and directed ourselves to Taiban.	y al Taibán nos dirijimos
They had given us information	Y los habían informado
that next day in the morning	que otro día por la mañana
they were going to disappear	se iban a desaparecer
to a land very distant.	para tierra muy lejana.
From the house of Brazil	De la casa de Brazil
we followed the tracks	la huella vamos tomando
each went a different way	sale cada uno a su rumbo
but gradually they came together.	y a poco se van juntando

We went on travelling two miles
always following the tracks.
Along the road of "Tul"
is where they went on travelling.

We reached the "casita"
of stone that is situated
a league from Taiban
on a barren hill.
In care of Roybal
we left the horses
in some old corrals
but we kept on as an advance
    guard.

Seven of us went with Pat Garrett
plowing up that snow
until seeing clearly the little house
and where it was situated.
We approached the little house
without any mishap befalling us,
and upon seeing the horses we
    knew
that the owners were within.

We stretched out in the snow
expected to see the
"Bilitos" and their peopple
come out—those we had come to
    fight.
We remained three hours in the
    same position
suffering a terrible cold
and with desperation.

When daylight had finally arrived
by the Grace of God
seven shots we fired
upon the body of Chas. Bowdre.
He was the first to show
certainly not expecting anything
in order to feed his horses
for Fate had decreed it so.

Caminabamos dos millas
siempre la huella siguiendo
Todo el camino del Tul
era el que ellos iban siguiendo.

Llegamos a la casita
de piedra que está situada
a una legue del Taibán
en una loma pelada.
Al cuidado de Roybal
dejamos la caballada
en unos corrales viejos
y seguimos avanzada.

Siete fuimos con Pat Garrett
arando aquella nevada
hasta ver bien la casita
y como estaba situada.
Acercámonos a la casita
sin tener ningún encuentro
y al ver las bestias supimos
que ellas estaban adentro.

En la nieve nos tendimos
esperando ver salir
a los Bilitos y su gente a quien
veníamos a combatir.
Nos estuvimos tres horas
en la misma posición
sufriendo un frio terrible
y con desesperación.

Cuando ya aclaro bien todo
por voluntad de Dios Padre
siete balasos tiramos
al cuerpo de Chas. Bowdre.
Fue el primero que salió
cierto sin esperar nada
a darles maiz a la bestias
pues su signo lo llamaba.

Eight yards distant from the house we remained reclining awaiting to have emerge the famouse "Bilito." It was then some one called from within, that his last words we might hear.	A ocho yardas de las casa estabamos agachados esperando que salieron los Bilitos afamados. Ya nos hublaron de adentro que Charley quería salir pues sus últimas palabras nos las quería decir.
Pat Garrett said to them that they must come out together with their hands raised or they would be dead men. But only Charley came out and even though badly wounded directed himself toward us with his hand uplifted.	Pat Garrett les respondió que salieran todos juntos con sus manos levantadas y si no serían difuntos. El Charley no más salió pues tenió malas heridas se dirigió hacia nosotros con sus manen levantadas.

He then took hold of Pat Garrett
and to speak to him made an
    effort
but he was unable to do it
having just then passed away.
After his demise
three horses we saw tied
and through the silence which was
    profound
it could be seen they were
    frightened.
	Ya se abrazó de Pat Garrett
	y el hablarle se esforzó
	pero ya no pudo hacerlo
	porque luego falleció.
	Despues de que ya murió
	tres bestias vimos atadas
	y por el silencio aunque profundo
	se veía que estaban espantadas.

To let them go free then Pat Garrett decided and sat down and with two well aimed shots the two halters he broke. The "Bilitos" on hearing this fire began to lead away by the halter the horse that remained.	El soltarlas determina Pat Garrett y se sentó y con dos finos balasos dos cabestros les cortó. Los "Biles" al oir los tiros empiezan a cabrestrear al caballo que quedó Queriéndolo hacer entrar.
Pat Garrett did not permit this having taken the whole thing in at a glance	Pat Garrett no permite esto pues toma una mira cierta le dió atras de la oreja

he struck him behind the ear
and he fell right at the very
   threshold
We heard the besieged
pounding on the inside
until it sounded like peals of
   thunder
but even so they could do nothing
and in vain they went on working.

Then we arose
from the place so cold,
for we almost froze to death
with our stomachs empty.
The composer saw himself
in great anxiety
in seeing his wings singed
but he did not "let up."

He was given an
assignment as sentinel
one afternoon while on a cliff
from the door of the house
he saw come forth a white flag
he sent word to his companions
we shouted for them to come out.
With hands up, we separated
   ourselves
Commanded as if by veterans.

Rudabaugh was the only one
to give himself up
his hands up in the air
which caused everyone to feel
   unspeakable joy.
Then came the announcement
they wished to give themselves up
if we should promise to see that
   they did not hang.

Pat Garrett consented
and accepted the condition
and sent the messenger

y cayó en la mera puerta
oimos a los sitiados
estar adentro golpeando
pues que ya se nos hacía
que dentro estaba tronando
pero aún con esto no podían
y en vano están trabajando.

Ya cuando nos levantamos
del lugareite frío
pues por poco nos helamos
con el estómago vacío.
El compositor se vió
en grande tribulación
al ver sus pies chamuscados
pero no dejó la acción.

Le tocó de centinela
en la tarde en un barranco
de la puerta de la casa
vió salir bandera blanca
Dio aviso a los compañeros
les gritamos que salieran
toditos nos dividimos
mandados por veteranos.

Rudabough no mas salió
con sus manos en el viento
lo cual a todos llenó
de indecible contento.

Nos dijo que ya querían
si acaso los protegían de
no ser solgados.

Pat Garrett les concedió
y afirmo la condición
y despacho al mensajero

to make the stipulations.	a que hicieran precision.
Then he saw them leave	Luego los vimos salir
the once famous house	de aquella afamada casa
with their hands upraised	con sus manos levantadas
red as coals.	Colorados como una brasa.
They asked us for food	Nos pidieron que comer
being hungry and thirsty	pues tenían buen apetito y sed,
for we had not permitted them	pues no los dejamos
to the little spring to descend.	que baharan al ojito.
Frank Stuart with Barney Viason	Frank Stewart con Barney Viason
and the composer took out	y el compositor sacaron
the fire-arms and cartridge pouches	las armas y cartucheras
that in the little house	que en la casita dejaron
the "Bilitos" had left	Los Biles al entregarse
upon giving themselves up.	pues ni un cartucho sacaron.
The names of the captives	Los nombres de los tomados
four remained alive	cuatro vivos que quedaron
are a little captivating	son un poco arrebatados
but they were taken prisoners.	pero presos se tomaron.
There were fifteen of us	
lest someone forget	Quince éramos los mentados
we let them ride behind us	que no nos dividarán.
in order to bring them to Taiban.	Nos los echamos a en ancas
	para traerlos al Tiabán.
Right there we twisted the neck of two,	
that of Dave Rudabaugh and Bilito	A dos allí mancornamos
with a short chain	a Dave Rudabaugh y el Bilito
we put a padlock on.	con una corta cadena
From there I separated myself	les echamos candadito.
But one thing I do know	De allí me separé yo
and that is that three were taken	pero una cosa si es
by Pat Garrett to Santa Fe.	que tres son los que llevó
	Pat Garrett a Santa Fé.
The capture of these men	
seemed very difficult	La tomado de estos hombres
that they would not be captured alive	muy difícil parecía
is what Bill was saying.	pues vivos no los tomaban
	era lo que el "Bil" decía.

William H. Bonney (Billy the Kid), taken at Fort Sumner sometime in 1880. According to Jon Tuska's caption for the frontispiece in his Billy the Kid: A Bio-Bibliography *(Greenwood Press, 1983), this famous tintype "is often reversed, placing the Kid's revolver on his left side," as it is here. Photo courtesy Museum of New Mexico, Neg. No. 30769.*

If Bill had known
that there was a reward
he would not have given himself
    up
and would have put up a fight.

Pat Garrett was the man
to whom we all owe
this great benefit
which we shall never forget.
The man himself is not small
he is not even unhandsome
He measures but six feet
plus some four inches.

And so, young men reflect,
the maxim of Pasquin
that you have listened to
and I have recorded here.
That he who travels fast
finds his career cut short
and before he knows it, finds
    himself
surrounded in his little house
just as the "Biles" were
    surrounded
and also their little gang.

I shall now take my leave
there being no reason not to do so
sufficient it is to say
that I'm from Puerto de Luna.

Si el "Bil" hubiera sabido
que habian una recompenza
él no se hubiera rendido
y hubiera hechoso defensa.

Pat Garrett ha sido el hombre
a quien todos le debemos
este gran beneficio
que nunca olvidaremos.
El hombre, chiquito no es,
no tiene feas miradas
no mido más que seis pies
con unas cuatro pulgadas.

El fín jóvenes reflejen
la maxima del pasquín
que ustedes han escuchado
y tienen escrito allí.
todo hombre que recio anda
su carrera en muy cortita
y antes que lo piense se halla
rodeado en una casita
como se hallaron los Biles
y toda su "Pacotita."

Despedida no les doy
porque no tengo ninguna
basta con saber que estoy
Aquí en el Puerto de Luna.[40]

►9◄

THE KID'S ESCAPE FROM
THE LINCOLN COUNTY JAIL

WILLIAM H. BONNEY WAS JAILED in Las Vegas on December 27, 1880, transported to Santa Fe by January 1, 1881, and held there until transferred to Mesilla on March 28. On April 10, 1881, he was convicted for murdering Sheriff William Brady, and on April 15 Judge Bristol sentenced him to be hung on May 13. Transported to Lincoln, where he was jailed on April 22, the Kid killed his two guards, J. W. Bell and Robert Olinger, when he made his now famous escape on April 28, 1881.[41]

ATTRIBUTED TO PAP JONES

COLLECTED BY KATHERINE RAGSDALE, 1936

In a land of restlessness, sorrow and happiness—New Mexico— there once lived a young man named William Bonney.

He lived during the time when arguments were settled with a gun—"survival of the fittest" was their motto.

This young boy was known as "Billy the Kid" and to some he was called an enemy, a ruthless killer, and to others a friend and hero.

"Billy the Kid" had as his friends the Jones family, Pap, Mam, John, Sam, Will. They had sheltered and fed him, treated him as one of their own and he never forgot their kindness to him.

It happened when "Billy the Kid" was in or near Lincoln, New Mexico, that John Jones was killed in Pierce Canyon by Bob Ollinger (said to be a cold blooded murder).

Several months passed and true to the western code "an eye

for an eye," Pap Jones (John's father) decided he would go to Lincoln where Ollinger was deputy sheriff and settle this debt.

It took Pap several days to make the trip in a wagon, and being hot and thirsty he went in a saloon for a drink. While he was in there who should walk in but "The Kid"— "What are you doing here?" asked Billy. "Why Kid I've come here to settle a debt with Ollinger." "Yes, I know Pap, he killed your son and my friend, but Pap you're too old to do this job, and anyway you're needed back home, I'll tell you what you do, you go out there, get in that wagon and start for home 'pronto,' and I'll take care of this job for you."

Reluctantly Pap left, but he knew he could depend on Billy to do the job.

On his way back home he stopped where the town of Artesia is now located and made an ox yoke (now in Mark Corbin's possession) and then went on to his home.

It was a week later he heard the news he was waiting for. "Billy the Kid" had been captured and sentenced to hang, but he made a daring escape from the Lincoln County Jail killing his guard and Ollinger.

The debt was paid.[42]

PACO ANAYA OF VAUGHN

COLLECTED BY EDITH L. CRAWFORD, N.D.

I was reading the other day where some writer was telling his readers about Billy the Kid riding 20 miles in a run on horseback "sideways," as it used to be called; that is, both feet and legs on one side of the horse.

The writer claimed Billy did this because he still had on the leg-irons which he had worn in jail.

This is not true. Why should he do this? He had practically the whole town of Lincoln at his command.

Before he killed his first deputy, named Bell, who was guarding him while a prisoner at the Lincoln County jail, he had the handcuffs off of one hand and after he had killed the second dep-

Lincoln, New Mexico, ca. 1886, showing Lincoln County Courthouse (until 1880 the Murphy-Dolan Store) in center foreground. Photo by J. R. Riddle. Courtesy Museum of New Mexico, Neg. No. 76100.

uty, Bob Ollenger, he crept down to a cook cabin, where old man Goss prepared the meals for the prisoners.

In those days nothing but wood was burned for fuel and like every old-time wood pile there was a log placed at the side for use in cutting wood stove length.

Well, the Kid crept up and said, "Dad Goss, I have a little, delicate job for you. I want you to cut these leg-irons in two."

He lay down on his back, placed his legs straddle of the log, with a cocked and drawn six shooter in his hand.

Old man Goss was standing in front of him with a drawn axe. Goss was an old man and a Texas Indian fighter. He wasn't afraid of anything. He was asked why he didn't kill the Kid with the drawn axe. He replied, "It couldn't be done. I believe the Kid would have gotten me. He was as fast as lightning.

"Furthermore," Goss continued, "I had a liking to the Kid. He was pleasant and nice to me and always complimented my jail cooking, and I never could see where Bob Ollenger was an asset to any commuunity. I came pretty near beating the Kid out of the job of killing Ollenger.

"Just a short time ago he and Garrett were over to the cook shack and Pat says: 'Dad, you don't seem to be armed. I know you are a good shot and in case of a jail break you could be a great help.'

"About that time Bob Ollenger butted in. He says, 'Pat, he don't need any gun. He is doing better work with his cooking. He is getting them in a slow way. I don't believe the strongest man in jail can stand his cooking 30 days.'

"I told him, 'you are one of those ignoramuses that was raised up on jerked beef and corn bread and trying to make people believe you are somebody. If you ever darken this door again, I'll shoot you. I'll split your head open with a skillet.' Yes, this country can easily spare such hombres as Ollenger."

The Kid said, "Dad, can you do the job? You want to be sure and hit the right place."

"Sure, Son," said Goss, "but I had rather you would raise that gun an inch or two. The blow might cause you to pull that thing off. Sabe?" The first stroke cut the irons in two and the Kid got up and said, "Dad, I hate to impose on good nature, but I'll have to ask you to get a bridle and go out there where the clerk's horse is grazing, catch him, and saddle him."

When this horse was caught and saddled the Kid mounted him and rode out of town, waving his hat.

He went straight to a plaza, 20 miles around the mountain, and got an old Mexican ranchman, who had a blacksmithing outfit, to take a coal chisel and cut the two pieces, which were welded around his legs.

After the Kid had changed mounts at Fort Sumner, he went to Arroyo Cibola, 12 miles below Fort Sumner, to the ranch of old man Anaya who had a large family of girls and only one boy, Paco, who was almost the same age as the Kid, both of them having been born in 1859. Paco Anaya is still at Vaughn, N.M., and was a member of the 12th Legislature. I give him credit for this valuable first hand information about the Kid, which I am using at this time.[43]

LADISLADO SALAS OF LINCOLN

COLLECTED BY EDITH L. CRAWFORD, 1937

I must have been at the age of seven or eight years, at the time Billy the Kid escaped from the Court House in Lincoln, we were living in the same place that I live now. I remember him very well as I went with my father Octavino Salas, about three times to the Court House where they had Billy the Kid, the day he escaped he stopped at our house. I remember well he had two sixshooters strapped across his shoulders and a rifle in his hand, he was riding sideways on a black horse. When I first saw him I got scared at seeing him with so many guns but he told me not to be afraid, that he wanted to see my father, this was about noon time. I was going out to where my father and some other men were working in the field, my father and the men arrived shortly, after talking with them a little while Billy the Kid told them that he had just killed two little Cotton Tail rabbits. He stayed for dinner at our hosue and my father helped him to get the shackles from his ankles. He had the hand cuffs in his pocket I know for he showed them to us.

Some say that Billy the Kid was a tall man but that is not so, he was a short man, with a black mustache. If you know my compadre Juan Zamora Gutierrez you have a pretty good idea what Billy the Kid looked like as he looks very much like the Kid.[44]

SAM FARMER OF CARRIZOZO

COLLECTED BY EDITH L. CRAWFORD, 1938

I have lived in Lincoln County sixty-eight years, which is all my life. I was born two miles west of Lincoln, New Mexico, on a ranch called "Henry's Ranch," named after my father, Henry Farmer. He filed on this place in 1865 and raised a few cattle and sheep and did some farming. He was married to Gavina Aguilar in 1865. Ten children were born to this union, seven boys and three girls. My oldest brother, Teodoro and myself are the only ones left of the Farmer family. Father was born in Missouri in 1842. His parents moved to Little Rock, Arkansas, when he was very small. He left home at the beginning of the Civil War at the age of eighteen. He roamed around for awhile and then came to Manzano, New Mexico. After staying there for a short while he came to Lincoln County in 1862 and lived on the Hughes place, which is located about one and one half miles below what is now the town of Tinnie, New Mexico. He worked for Mr. Hughes for quite some time and then he filed on a homestead two miles west of Lincoln, New Mexico. His place was on the Rio Bonito and he used the water for irrigating a small farm. He used to freight some and during the years that Murphy and Dolan and McSween and Tunstall had their stores in Lincoln he hauled freight for them and also for J. C. De Laney of Fort Stanton, New Mexico. He had two teams of oxen, six to a team and had two big freight wagons. He hauled from Las Vegas to Lincoln and Fort Stanton. He was never bothered by the Indians but once. He was coming from Picacho to Lincoln, New Mexico, driving two mules and a band of Indians attacked him. He was shot three times with arrows. Once in the upper left arm, in the left shoulder and leg. The mules got frightened and ran away and Father always said that is the only thing that saved his life.

Father always used the oxen in freighting and it took them from twenty-eight to thirty-five days to make a round trip from Lincoln to Las Vegas and return and that depended on the weather. We were living on our ranch during the Lincoln County War but our family took no part in it. We all liked Billy the Kid and would do anything that we could for him. Once my father took myself and my two older brothers to one of the trials of Billy the Kid. He wanted to impress upon our young minds that no one could break the laws as he did and not pay the penalty.

The day that Billy the Kid killed Bell and Olinger, my father, two brothers and myself were irrigating our wheat field when Billy came riding by on a black horse. He stopped and hollered, "Hello, Henry." Father looked up and said, "Hello Billy, what are you doing here?" Billy replied, "I am going, I don't think you will see me any more. I killed two men at the Courthouse and I am on my way, good-bye." He kicked his horse and went off up the road as fast as he could go. I remember distinctly seeing the shackles on his legs. That was the last time we ever saw Billy the Kid. My brothers and myself always liked Billy the Kid so much for he always took time to talk and play with us when we saw him. Billy was killed at Fort Sumner about six weeks later by Pat Garrett.

My father lived in Lincoln County until his death in 1898 and was buried in Lincoln. My mother was born in the Manzano mountains at a place called Chato in 1848. She died in 1893 and was buried in Lincoln. Father was a very quiet unassuming man and a good law abiding citizen.[45]

COLLECTED BY EDITH L. CRAWFORD, 1937

I remember very well when Billy the Kid killed Bell and Olinger I was irrigating wheat with my father and older brother, it was about one o'clock I guess.

I saw a man coming riding a black horse and he rode down by the ditch where we were working and stopped. He hollered to my father, "Hello Henry!" My father said, "What you doing here Bill?"

He said, "I am going, I don't think you'll see my any more." My father said, "Why Bill," and he said, "I killed two men at the court house and I'm trying to get away, good-bye."

(Answers to questions I asked him)

When he came by the ditch he was riding straddle.

He was straight and slender and walked very quick. He had light brown hair and green eyes and he wore a cowboy hat with the brim straight in front and turned up in the back. It was always on the side of his head. I never saw him with a cap or a black hat one, always it was a light hat. He was about 20 I guess.

I never saw him with a girl in Lincoln and never heard of his having one there, but I heard that he had a Spanish girl at Bosque Grande named Carolina.

I remember the Lincoln County war, not much, but the shooting and the soldiers. I remember Billy well. I liked him. I was around 11 I guess. His mother was living then. He spoke of her to my father and to Hijinio Salazar for both of them told me so. He talked to Hijinio about her during the Lincoln County War.

(Stories by Sam Farmer)

I used to go with my father often when he freighted with a team of oxen. We used to stop at a camp which was on the road between Las Vegas and Lincoln near the Gallinas mountains. We used to see Billy there. I remember once I saw him and he was eating his dinner. He used to sit with his legs straight out with his plate on his lap and his hat on his boots. I remember I asked him, "What you set that way for?" and he said, "That's a quick way to get up if I have to."

One of Billy's compadres was a man named Apolonio Sedillo. Once I was at a house of María de la Antilles and I started to go in a room. She stopped me quick and said, "Get away from that room coyote." The bed had a sheet up all around it so nobody could see who was in the bed. Apolonio was in there sitting against the wall, Billy was in the bed. That was when Billy was on the dodge after the war.

(Told Me by Hijinio Salazar)

A story about Billy that Hijinio told me was about a man named Mike. I don't remember his other name. Mike talked too much about Billy. He said he was going to kill Billy the first time that he saw him. One day Billy came to the saloon in Lincoln. Mike was there. Billy said, "Hello Mike. Come on and have a drink, maybe that will be the last drink we'll have together." When they got their drink Billy had his in his left hand. He said, "Pull your gun Mike, you'll need it for I'm going to kill you or you me." He shot Mike right there. Billy didn't bother anybody unless they were out to get him. If he was your friend he was your friend but he was hard on anybody who talked about getting him if he knew it.

(Told Me by Apolonio Sedillo)

Once Billy and Sedillo stole all the horses, mules and burros that the Indians had. The Indians were about three miles above Fort Stanton then. They could not get them all at once but they did not have very much trouble except for one old horse mule. The Indians tied a rope on the mule's neck and took the rope inside the teepee. The Indians had a little pup that barked every time that they would get close. One nite Billy took a half a sack of sopapillas with him and every time the dog barked he'd throw a sopapilla to

64

*Eugenio Salazar (born February 14, 1863; died January 7, 1936) in the
1920s. Photo courtesy Special Collections, University of Arizona Library.*

him and he went up to the mule and cut the rope with his knife.
Every time the dog barked he'd throw another sopapilla to him. He
finally got the mule and rode him away. Billy and Sedillo drove all
the horses and mules and burros to the Chisum Ranch below
Roswell.

(Told Me by Gregorio Ventura)

One time Billy went across the border to Chihuahua. He went
to a gambling house and held up a Monte game and put all the
money in a sack and came back across the border. He had a lot of
money and he did not kill anybody.

These stories were told to me by Sam Farmer who lived in Lincoln during and after the Lincoln County War and knew Billy the
Kid.[46]

►10◄

THE LINCOLN COUNTY WAR
AND THE KID'S DEATH

MANY OLD-TIMERS TOLD A RANGE of reminiscences about the so-called Lincoln County War of 1869 to 1881. Most of their memories center around Billy the Kid's part in these events.[47]

FRANK B. COE OF GLENCOE

LETTER TO WILLIAM STEELE DEAN, 1926

Mr. Dean. My Dear Sir:

I was surprised to hear from you, one I never knew. But I am proud of you, the good feeling you have for Billy the Kid. He was the most noted character that New Mexico ever knew. He killed several of the most noted outlaws that ran in this part of N.M. All the men he killed got just what was coming to them. I never knew him to shoot a man in the back. He did not fear any man if he would meet him face to face. He went through the Lincoln County War in -78, was in every battle we had, was one of the best soldiers we had, always in the lead. He was slightly wounded when sheriff Brady was killed in Lincoln. Kid went over the adobe wall in the middle of the street to get his fire arms. Some one fired from a porthole and shot him in the side, a slight wound. He got all the arms and cartridges off then went over the wall to safety. Billy was then about 17, 5 ft. 8 in., weight 138 lb. stood straight as an Indian, fine looking a lad as I ever met. He was a Lady's Man, the Mex girls were crazy about him. He spoke their language well. He was a fine dancer, could go all their gates (gaits) and was one of them. Mr. Burns, the author of the saga, didn't give him near the credit he deserved. The more I think of him the bigger he gets in my mind. With no people to back him up he had to fight for his life.

He was a wonder, you would have been proud to have known him.

George Coe is a cousin of mine and was through the war with us. Has a good farm and lives near me. If I ever meet you I could tell you one desperate deed after another where the Kid came through with honors. I am sending here one of his pictures. It does not give him the credit it should.

As ever, FRANK B. COE.[48]

FRANCISCO TRUJILLO OF SAN PATRICIO

COLLECTED BY EDITH L. CRAWFORD, 1937

I arrived at San Patricio in the year 1877. During the first days of October, sheriff Brady appointed a committee to pursue some bandits whom we found at Harry Baker's ranch at Siete Rios. There we arrested them and brought them to jail at Lincoln.

In November the people of Penasco went to take the bandits out from jail. Among the people coming from Penasco, was Billy the Kid. At about the same time Francisco Trujillo, my brother Juan Trujillo and I went to Pajarito to hunt deer. We were at the mouth of the Pajarito Canyon skinning deer, when we saw two persons passing. One was Frank Baker, the other was Billy Mote. One was a bandit and the other a body guard whom Marfe [Murphy] kept at the ranch. The last one was a thief also. When they passed my brother said, "Let us get away quickly, these are bad people." So, we got our horses, saddled them and left in the direction of San Patricio. On the way we met the bandits and the people who were coming from the jail at Lincoln.

The bandits surrounded Juan, my brother. I started to get away but Billy the Kid followed me telling me to stop. I then turned around and saw that he was pointing a rifle at me so I jumped from my horse and aimed my gun at him. He then went back to where the people were and aimed his gun at Juan saying, "If Francisco does not surrender I am going to kill you." Lucas Gallegos then shouted, "Surrender, friend, otherwise they will kill my *compadre* Juan." Billy then took my gun from where I had laid it and we returned to the place where the people were. Billy then said to me, "We have exchanged guns now let us exchange saddles." I said that suited me, picking up the gun when another Texan said, "Hand it over you don't need it." At this point Lucas Gallegos interposed saying to my brother, "Let me have the pistol, *compadre*." Then my brother gave Lucas the pistol in its holster. Then and there we parted and left for San Patricio to recount our experiences.

In December Macky Swin [McSween] and Marfe went to court about a guardianship and a decision was rendered in favor of Macky Swin. When Marfe saw that he had lost out he ordered his men to get Macky Swin or some of his companions. Macky Swin hearing of the order that Marfe had given gathered his people in order to protect himself. Among those he rounded up was Billy the Kid, Charley Barber and Macky Nane [McKinney]. In addition to these three men, six more got together and Macky Swin made them the same promise to the effect that a prize of $500 was to be awarded to each person who killed one of the Marfes. It was then and there that Billy the Kid organized his people and went out in search of Frank Baker and Billy Mote whom he apprehended on the other side of the Pecos River and brought to Lincoln where it was planned to execute them. Later when they talked it over further with the rest, it was again decided to kill them but not to bring them to Lincoln. One of the gang named McLoska [McCloskey] said that he preferred to be shot himself rather than to have one of those men killed. No sooner had he said this, when he found himself shot behind the ear. After they killed McLoska, Frank Baker and Billy Mote were promptly executed. From there Billy's gang left for San Patricio where Billy asked for Francisco Trujillo in order to deliver back to him his gun. It was here that they hired a Mexican boy to go to Lincoln for provisions and to collect the reward that Macky Swin had promised for the Marfes whom they had just killed.

A few days later Macky Nane, Frank Coe and Alex Coe were on their way to Picacho from Lincoln. When they reached the Ojo Ranch they were confronted by the Marfes. They made Frank Coe prisoner and shot Alex Coe in the leg, while the Indian, Juan Armijo, ran after Macky Nane and killed him. By order of Robert Baker, Macky Nane had been the leader whom Macky Swin had had for a guard. Within a few days a complaint was sworn against the Indian, Juan Armijo, and sheriff Brady deputized Jose Chaves to arrest him. Chaves then named seven men, beside himself in order that they should go with him to look for Armijo and he in turn deputized eight Americans and eight Mexicans and altogether they left for Siete Rios where they found Juan across the Pecos River, as well as two other Texans.

When Atanasio Martinez, John Scroggin, Billy the Kid and I arrived at the door of the hut, Juan Armijo spoke up and said, "How are you Kiko?" "Come on out," I said to Juan. "You have killed Macky Nane," to which he nodded in assent but adding that it was by order of Robert Baker under threat of being prosecuted himself, should he fail to carry out instructions. I then made my way to Macky Nane who had been hiding behind some tree trunks in an effort to defend himself against those who were shooting at the house, and killed him.

When we left the hut, accompanied by Juan, he said to me, "Don't let them kill me Kiko!" Seeing a string of people coming from Siete Rios, we ran to a nearby hill and from there towards the plains and then headed for Roswell, on the other side of the Pecos River, and came out two miles below at Gurban. It was here that Billy the Kid, Jose Chaves y Chaves, and Stock proposed to kill the Indian Armijo. I said to Chaves, "Is it not better to take him in and let the law have its course?" Charley Barber then came up to me and said, "Come on Francisco, let us be running along."

As I came up to Charley, I turned and saw the Indian Armijo riding between them very slowly. When Charley and I had gone about fifty yards we noticed that the Indian had gotten away from his captors and was riding away as fast as he could. Billy the Kid and Jose Chaves took out after him and began to shoot at him until they got him. Several of us congregated at the place where he fell.

Billy the Kid then said to me, "Francisco, here are the saddle and trappings that I owe you." I then commanded Esiquio Sanchez to do me the favor of bringing me the horse the Indian Armijo had been riding, in order that I might remove the saddle which was covered with blood. Noting my disgust Doke said that he would take it and clean it and let me have his in the meantime. And so, we exchanged. Our business finished we turned homeward and crossed the river at a point called "Vado de los Indios." At Gurban, this side of the Pecos River we slept. In the morning we arose and went to Aleman to have breakfast. There we found Macky Swin at John Chisum's ranch. Breakfast being over Macky Swin told us to go into the store and take anything that we wished. At this point it was decided to leave Captain Stock to guard over Macky Swin. Of the original eight Mexicans in the party, four were left to join the Americans, not having admitted the other four to do so. Macky Swin then asked us to meet him the following Monday at Lincoln because said he, "As soon as I arrive, Brady is going to try and arrest me and you should not let him get away with it. If I am arrested I shall surely be hung and I don't want to die, while if you kill Brady you shall earn a reward."

From Aleman we left for Berendo where we found a *fandango* in progress. We were enjoying ourselves very thoroughly when Don Miguel came up to us and said, "Better be on your way boys because presently there will arrive about fifty Marfes who are probably coming here to get you." Esteco, our leader, agreeing with Don Miguel, commanded us to saddle our horses. We had not been gone half a mile when we heard shouts and gun-shots so we decided to wait for the gang and have it out. Our efforts were of no avail, however, as the gang failed to show up. We then pursued our course toward the Capitan Mountains and arrived at Agua Negra at day break and there we had our lunch. At this point the party broke up, the Anglos going to Lincoln, the Mexicans to San Patricio whence they arrived on Sunday afternoon. Billy the Kid then said to Jose Chaves, "Let us draw to see who has to wait for Macky Swin tomorrow at Lincoln. The lots fell to Charley Barber, John Milton and Jim French White, whereupon the leader decided that all nine Anglos should go. Bill said that it was best for none of the Mexican boys to go and when Chaves protested saying that the Anglos were no braver than he, Bill explained that Brady was married to a Mexican and that it was a matter of policy, all Mexicans being sentimental about their own. Chaves being appeased urged the rest to go on promising to render assistance should a call come for help. A Texan named Doke said that since his family was Mexican too, he would remain with the others. Stock then gave orders to proceed. The horses were saddled and they left for Lincoln. Doke, Fernando Herrera, Jesus Sais and Candelario Hidalgo left for Ruidoso. The next morning Don Pancho Sanches left for Lincoln to make some purchases at the store. Being in the store about eleven, the mail arrived and with it Macky Swin. There also arrived Brady and a Texan named George Hamilton. At this juncture Brady also arrived where he found Billy the Kid, Jim French, Charley Barber and John Melton. They were in the corral from whence two of the gang shot at one, and two others at the other, where they fell.

Billy the Kid then jumped to snatch Brady's rifle and as he was leaning over someone shot at him from a house they used to call "El Chorro." Macky Swin then reached the house where the nine Macky Swins were congregated—the four who were in the corral and five who had been at the river. There they remained all day until nightfall and then proceeded to San Patricio. The next morning they proposed going to the hills should there be a war and so that it could be waged at the edge of town and in order not to endanger the lives of the families living there. The same day, toward evening, six Mexicans came to arrest Macky Swin. They did not arrive at the Plaza but camped a little further down between the acequia and the river at a place where there were thick brambles. Shortly after the Mexicans arrived Macky Swin came with his people to eat supper at the house of Juan Trujillo—that being their headquarters, that also being their mess hall, having hired a negro to prepare meals. After supper they scattered among the different houses, two or three in each house. In one of these at the edge of town Macky Swin and an American boy whose name was Tome locked themselves in. Next day early in the norming the six Mexicans who had been looking for Macky Swin showed up. When they arrived at the house where Macky Swin was, Tome came out and shot at the bunch of Mexicans and hit Julian Lopez in the arm. They then fled to the top of a near-by hill. An hour having passed from the time that Tome shot Julian, about forty Marfes came down to San Patricio killing horses and chickens. At this point there arrived two Marfes, an American and a Mexican. The American's name was Ale Cu, and the Mexican's Lucio Montoya. When the Macky Swins became aware of them, they began to fire and killed all the horses. The two Marfes ran away to San Patricio where the rest of the Marfes were tearing down a house and taking out of the store everything that they could get hold of. From there all the Marfes went to Lincoln and for about a month nothing of interest occurred.

I don't recall exactly when Macky Swin, who was being hounded down by the Marfes, was killed but I do remember that he gathered together all his friends and went back home to Lincoln accompanied by eight Mexicans and two Americans, also his wife. When the Marfes found out that he was in the house they surrounded him but seeing that they were unable to hurt him they caused to be brought over a company of soldiers and a cannon from the nearby Fort. Notwithstanding this Macky Swin instructed his people not to fire. For this reason the soldiers had to wait until it was dark. The Marfes then set fire to the house and the soldiers returned to the fort. When the first room burned down, Ginio Salazar and Ignacio Gonzales came out to the door but the Marfes knocked them down and left them there, dazed. When the flames reached the middle room, an American proposed to go out through the doors of the kitchen on the north side. No sooner did he jump than the Marfes knocked him down. Francisco Samora jumped also and he too was shot. Vicente Romero was next and there the three remained in a heap. It was then proposed by Billy the Kid and Jose Chaves y Chaves to take aim at the same time and shoot, first to one side then to the other. Chaves took Macky Swin by the arm and told him to go out to which Macky Swin answered by taking a chair and placing it in the corner stating that he would die right there. Billy and Jose Chaves then jumped to the middle door, one on one side, and the other on the other. Then Robert Baker and a Texan jumped and said, "Here is Macky Swin." Drawing out his revolver he shot him three times in the breast. When the last shot was fired Billy the Kid said, "Here is Robert," and thrust a revolver in his mouth while Jose Chaves shot at the Texan and hit him in the eye. Billy and Chaves then went along the river headed for San Patricio where they both remained for some time.

In October the Governor accompanied by seven soldiers and other persons came to San Patricio camping. Having heard about the exploits of Billy the Governor expressed a desire to meet him and sent a messenger to fetch him. The interview was in the nature of a heart to heart talk wherein the Governor advised Billy to give up his perilous career. At this point occurred the general election and George Kimbrall was elected sheriff of the county. Obeying the Governor's orders he called out the militia having commissioned Sr. Patron as captain and Billy the Kid as First Lieutenant. During that year—that of '79 things were comparatively quiet and Billy led a very uneventful life.

About the last part of October of the same year, the Governor issued an order that the militia should make an effort to round all bandits in Chaves County, a task which the militia was not able to accomplish hence it disbanded. Billy the Kid received an honorable discharge and would probably have gone straight from then on had it not been that at this juncture the District Court met and the Marfes swore a complaint against him and ordered sheriff Kimbrall to arrest him. Billy stubbornly refused to accompany the sheriff and threatened to take away his life rather than to be apprehended. Again nothing was heard for a time and then Pat Garrett offered to bring in the desperado for a reward. The Governor having been made aware of this situation himself offered a reward of $500. Immediately Pat Garrett accompanied by four other men got ready to go after Billy and found him and three other boys, whom they surrounded. One morning, during the siege, one of Billy's companions went out to fetch a pail of water whereupon Pat Garrett shot at him, as well as the others, hitting him in the neck and thereby causing him to drop the pail and to run into the house. With a piece of cloth, Billy was able to dress the wound of the injured man and at least stop the hemorrhage. He then advised the wounded man to go out and to pretend to give himself up, hiding his fire-arm but using it at the first opportune moment to kill Pat. Charley did as he was told but when he went to take aim, dropped dead. Billy and the other three companions were kept prisoners for three days but finally hunger and thirst drove them out and caused them to venture forth and to give themselves up. Billy was arrested, there being no warrant for the others. Then followed the trial which resulted in a sentence to hang within thirty days. News of the execution having spread about people began to come in for miles around to be present on the fatal day but Billy was not to afford them that much pleasure having escaped three days before the hanging.

A deputy and jailer had been commissioned to stand guard over him. On the day of the escape at noon the jailer told the deputy to go and eat his dinner and that he would then go himself and fetch the prisoner's. It was while the jailer and Billy remained alone that the prisoner stepped to the window to fetch a paper. He had somehow gotten rid of his handcuffs and only his shackles remained. With the paper in his hand he approached the officer and before the latter knew what his charge was up to, yanked his revolver away from him and the next instant he was dead. Billy lost no time in removing his keeper's cartridge belt as well as a rifle and a "44 W.C.F." which were in the room.

When the deputy heard the shots he thought that the jailer must have shot Billy who was trying to escape and ran from the hotel to the jail on the steps of which he met Billy who said "hello" as he brushed past him, firing at him as he dashed by. Billy's next move was to rush to the hotel and to have Ben Esle remove his shackles. He also provided for him a horse and saddled it for Billy upon the promise that he was to leave it at San Patricio. True to his word Billy secured another horse at San Patricio from his friend Juan Trujillo promising in turn to return the same as soon as he could locate his own.

Billy now left San Patricio and headed for John Chisum's cattle ranch. Among the cowboys there, there was a friend of Billy Mote who had sworn to kill the Kid wherever he found him in order to avenge his friend. But Billy did not give him time to carry out his plan, killing him on the spot. From there Billy left for

Berendo where he remained a few days. Here he found his own horse and immediately sent back Juan Trujillo's. From Berendo Billy left for Puerto de Luna where he visited Juan Patron, his former captain. Patron did everything to make his and his companion's stay there as pleasant as possible. On the third evening of their stay there was to have been a dance and Billy sent his companion to make a report of what he saw and heard. While on his way there, and while he was passing in front of some abandoned shacks, Tome was fired upon by one of Pat Garrett's men and killed. No sooner had Billy heard the distresing news than he set out for the house of his friend Pedro Macky [McKee] at Bosque Grande where he remained in hiding until a Texan named Charley Wilson, and who was supposed to be after Billy, arrived. The two exchanged greetings in a friendly fashion and then the stranger asked Billy to accompany him to the saloon, which invitation Billy accepted. There were six or seven persons in the saloon when the two entered. Drinks were imbibed in and a general spirit of conviviality prevailed when some one suggested that the first one to commit a murder that day was to set the others up. "In that case the drinks are on me," said Charley who commanded all to drink to their heart's content. Billy then ordered another round of drinks and by this time Charley who was feeling quite reckless began to shoot at the glasses not missing a single one until he came to Billy's. This he pretended to miss, aiming his shot at Billy instead. This gave Billy time to draw out his own revolver and before Charley could take aim again, Billy had shot the other in the breast twice. When he was breathing his last, Billy said, "Do not whimper you were too eager to buy those drinks." It was Billy's turn now to treat the company.

Quiet again reigned for a few days. In the meantime Pat Garrett was negotiating with Pedro Macky for the deliverance of Billy. When all details were arranged for, Pat left for Bosque Grande secretly. At the ranch house, Pedro hid Pat in a room close beside the one Billy was occupying. Becoming hungry during the night Billy got up and started to prepare a lunch. First he built a fire, then he took his hunting knife and was starting to cut off a hunk of meat from a large piece that hung from one of the *vigas* when he heard voices in the adjoining room. Stepping to the door he partially opened it and thrusting his head in asked Pedro who was with him. Pedro replied that it was only his wife and asked him to come in. Seeing no harm in this Billy decided to accept the invitation only to be shot in the pit of the stomach as he stood in the door. Staggering back to his own room it was not definitely known that the shot had been fatal until a cleaning woman stumbled over the dead body upon entering the room the following morning.[49]

CAROLATTA BACA BRENT OF SILVER CITY

COLLECTED BY FRANCES E. TOTTY, 1938

When anyone enters the house of Mrs. James Brent they wonder if the home isn't a doll house. The home is very interesting with statues and other symbols of the Catholic faith. The place looks more as a home where someone spends hours at play than a home for adults, everything is in place and seems so real that one could spend hours just admiring the house. Mrs. Brent in keeping with her home resembles a black headed Spanish dressed doll with high top shoes on. She is about 53 inches tall and probably weighs eighty pounds. Her eyes sparkling she meets her guests with a smile of "Welcome."

When the name of Billie the Kid is mentioned Mrs. Brent begins to talk in broken English with such enthusiasm that you sit spell bound until she finishes her story.

Mrs. Brent says about Lincoln County: "Lincoln County before the war was a thriving cattle country with Lincoln as its trading center for miles around. People came from as far as Mesilla to the dances, but after the war the town was a thing of the past as far as ever amounting to anything. The last time that I was there it was as it was the day the war was over only a little more decayed.

"Mr. McSween, Sheriff Brady, and others that lost their lives in the war weren't bad men, but as at that time the gun was the real law, and they crossed someone they were disposed of by the gun. Jimmie Dolan, Young Riley, Billie the Keed, and other men

"The Finale—The Kid Killed by the Sheriff at Fort Sumner," July 14, 1881. Photo courtesy Museum of New Mexico, Neg. No. 47640.

that lived by the quick draw of their gun weren't really mean men, for they never killed unless their lives were at stake; they weren't murders, but men of the frontier days.

"Today The Keed is featured as a mean man, as black as a Mexican, he wasn't he was a light complected boy that was always smiling; he was brave and loyal to his friends.

"Pat Garrett had been a friend of The Keed's, but after the war he was made sheriff of Lincoln, and it fell his duty to arrest The Keed. Mr. Garrett with several deputies among them my husband James Brent arrested him the first time at Stinking Springs.

"Mr. Garrett was tipped off that The Keed was at Stinking Springs and before day break he and his deputies surrounded the house.

"Garrett tried to get The Keed to surrender, but the boy refused saying, 'Pat I may show you a trick or two yet.' To which Garrett replied, 'Billie you can't escape for we have you surrounded, and you can't get away.'

"'Pat, you don't know I may get away yet.'

"The Keed's horse was tethered outside of the hut he was in, and the boy began to pull the rope to get the horse in the house, but Mr. Garrett quickly caught on to the boy's plan and shot the rope into letting the horse get away. The Kid was now on foot as well as surrounded, he hadn't had anything to eat for several days and was cold. Mr. Garrett sent after food for his men and the food was probably why the boy surrendered when he did for when he smelled the coffee he called to Mr. Garrett: 'Pat have a heart and send over a pot of coffee.'

"Garrett replied, 'Come and get it Keed; coffee sure is good in this kind of weather.'

"'Pat, today is my birthday, and can't you send me some coffee.'

"The reply was 'Keed come after it with your hands up and you can have all the coffee you want.'

After a few minutes the Keed called back, 'Pat I'll come if you will promise not to shoot me when I come out at the door.'

"'I promise Billie.' Mr. Garrett was glad to make the promise as he didn't want to kill The Keed as they were friends.

"The Keed came out with his hands raised, and was made a prisoner. He was taken to Lincoln then to Santa Fe. Later he was sent to Mesilla for trial where he was convicted of killing Sheriff Brady and brought back to Lincoln to be hanged.

"While the boy was in the Lincoln jail; he was always cheerful he could be seen walking back and forth in the jail whistling.

"He was playing cards with the jailer and knocked a card off the table. When his jailer stooped to get the card, Billie reached over and took the jailer's gun. He was handcuffed, but he was brave enough to make a trial of escaping against odds. The boy escaped and no one in Lincoln tried to keep him from going as they all knew he could shoot too good to risk their lives to stop him.

"A few minutes after the boy's escape the streets were full of people, but they soon were back in their homes with the doors closed until he left town.

"The Keed went to Fort Sumner to the Maxwell home, many said to capture the daughter of Pete Maxwell and take to Mexico with him. Mr. Garrett heard that he was in Fort Sumner and went over to see if he could find him. Billie was at the home of Celesa Gutierrez. He had come in from the sheep camp and was hungry Celesa was going to get a steak off of Maxwell's porch, but Billie insisted in getting it for her, and went across the yard in his stocking feet after the meat.

"He went into Pete's bedroom where Garrett had gone only a few minutes before. He asked 'quien es?' His answer was a shot from Garrett's gun. Garrett recognized the Keed when he spoke and from the silhouette in the doorway as he came into the room.

"The Keed was gone but many Spanish girls mourned for him. He was buried in Hell's Half Acre an old military graveyard. His grave isn't marked and few people know where it is in the cemetery."[50]

JOSH BRENT OF SILVER CITY

COLLECTED BY FRANCES E. TOTTY, 1938

My grandfather Sotorona Baca and his wife were born in Barcelona, Spain, and was considered quite wealthy for those days. They came to America and settled at El Paso, Texas, where they lived for some time but the old Spanish legend was going the rounds at the time that they settled at El Paso and it wasn't long until he decided that there was something to the story, and invested $10,000 in the swindling scheme, which was all lost as the people that he gave the money to were imposters of the early days and the old story of the lost bullion has gone on down the years.

Grandfather after he lost so much money moved to Lincoln and bought a ranch or two as he figured that he was nearly broke and he had to recover some of his losses. He started to raise cattle, horses and mules and hogs. He had been a captain in the army and was hired by the government to take supplies to the Fort Stanton Reservation. He never did have any trouble in getting the supplies to the Indians as Murphy was hired by the government to furnish the supplies.

My mother Carolotta Baca Brent was born in Lincoln on Jan.

79

17, 1865. She has a sister that still lives in Lincoln. Mother was in the middle of the Lincoln War and carried messages for both parties. The message was delivered in a bucket of beans. Mother saw Billie the Kid kill Sheriff Brady from the window in the tower. The Spanish and Mexican class of people were friends to Billie the Kid. They often hid him under the floor of their houses and in every way possible warned him of his dangers.

My father was an under sheriff of Pat Garrett's and was with him when he captured Billie the Kid at Stinking Springs.

Pat Garrett told father after he killed Billie the Kid that a fellow from the east wrote to him and said that he would pay $500 for the trigger finger of the boy. I have read many books on the boy, but this is one fact that I have never seen published. Billie the Kid was not a killer but was fighting for a cause and father told us that he was an unusually nice boy. He took the part of McSween and fought for McSween's right to the finish. Mr. McSween was a very refined gentleman and never could believe that the guns should rule as they did, and could never be convinced that he should carry a gun. He died in the war carrying his Bible. Mrs. McSween was a beautiful lady, and understood the ways of the world much better than her husband who was an idealist.

Emerson Huff was living in Lincoln in the early days. He worked around the town at anything that he could get to do. He wanted to save enough money to get to Kansas City. Father was going to take some prisoners to Fort Leavenworth and told Mr. Huff that he would take him that far as a guard. He left father at Leavenworth and drifted into Louisiana and there wrote Mississippi Bubble which brought him a small fortune.

I have at home a spool made into a toy by Pat Garrett that he gave to me when I was a youngster. Pat Garrett after killing Billie the Kid always said that he sure hated to kill the boy, but he knew that it was either his life or the boy's life, and as he was sent out to bring him back he did the only thing he could do for he realized that Billie would never be taken alive again.[51]

►11◄

THE DEATH OF BILLY THE KID

SHERIFF PAT GARRETT SHOT BILLY THE KID on the night of July 14, 1881, in the bedroom of Pete Maxwell's Fort Sumner house.[52]

JOHN ALLRED

COLLECTED BY FRANCES E. TOTTY, 1938

I was born in March 1875, just out of Lincoln in Lincoln County. The people living outside of Lincoln didn't take active part in the Lincoln County War, but most of them sided one way or the other. My parents were for the McSween faction of the fight. We always felt that the McSweens were fighting for a cause. Father went to Billie the Kid's funeral and he has often said, that even though many have said that the Kid was not dead, he knew for a fact that it was The Kid that Pat Garrett killed.

Billie the Kid was an A-1 fellow, loved by everyone that knew him. We all felt that it was a dirty, cowardly trick for Pat Garrett to pull when he killed the boy. Billie had been a friend to Pat Garrett when he first came to Lincoln County, even furnishing the man with a horse, then after the war was over and the government wanted a man to capture the boy, Garrett was willing to take the job of capturing the man that had been his friend, the man that he knew all of his friends and hide-outs. The Greer Brothers, John Holder, and the Gilmores were all friends of the Kid's, they all grieved when the Kid was killed. The boy was a killer no doubt, but he also was a real friend to those that he loved. Billie never killed a man without a cause, as far as him getting out and killing for the love of killing he did not do anything of the kind, he never killed a man unless his life was in danger or the life of some of his friends.

In the war The Kid was fighting for a cause, for McSween and others of the McSween party had been a real friend to the boy and he always took the part of a friend. It was not the boy's desire to fight that made him go into the war, but a sense of loyalty.[53]

BALLAD: DEATH OF THE FAMOUS "BILITO"

MUERTE DEL AFAMADO BILITO

COLLECTED AND TRANSLATED
BY AURORA LUCERO WHITE,
1936

The famous "Bilito"
on account of punishment
    well deserved
was jailed at Santa Fe.
Indebted to society for the lives of
    twenty
from Santa Fe to Mesilla
it was necessary he be taken
He was very happy seeing that it
    meant a trip.

The Court did not hesitate
and accordingly he was sentenced,
and on the 13th of May
he was to be hanged.
But circumstances so change,
        also propositions
that many were those who felt
    anguish
at seeing the sentence executed
although deserved by the robbers.

But I shall go on with my story
as long as it has been commenced
for it is sufficiently notorious
not to have it condensed.

El Bilito mentado
por penas bien merecidas
fué en Santa Fe encarcelado.
Deudor de veinte en vida
de Santa Fe a la La Mesilla
requerido fué llevarlo.
El tuvo mucha alegría
vienda que era por pasearlo.

La Corte no tuvo fallo
pues fué por deber, juzgado
y el día trece de Mayo
tenía que ser colgado.
Mas, cambian las circunstancias
también las proposiciones
que muchas fueron las ansias
de los nobles corazones
ejecutar la sentencia
que merecen los ladrones.
Pero sequiré mi historia
siendo que esta comenzada
pues es bastante notoria
pa no ser olvidada.

From where Bill was sentenced,
    and justly so,
he was transported to Lincoln
and locked up in prison
to await the fatal day of the
    execution.
There were present
Bill Ollinger, the deputy,
and also Bell, as assistants.
They were sentenced
with strict orders, no doubt
to watch over the sentenced-one
without any partiality.

Bell had to remain there alone,
while Bob went to supper
for the awaited hour was
    approaching
and Bill, not being asleep,
takes advantage of the opportunity
and soon makes up his mind
to gain his liberty.

Having handcuffs,
two in one hand,
with all his energy he struck a blow
    so fierce
that Bell fell in cold blood
without his God acclaiming.
With Bell's pistol and with one
    shot
he put an end to the act so cruel
and then, he prepared himself.

When Bob was eating his supper
he heard a shot resound
and hastened quickly
without finishing his food
He scarcely crossed the line
where he was to remain
for there Bill shot him
before he had time to arrive.

De donde fué sentenciado
el "Bil" por justa razón
a Lincóln fué transportado
y encerrado en la prision
a esperar al día dado
para ser su ejecución.
Bil Ollinger diputado
y también Bell para ayuda
fueron allí estacionados
con estricta órden, sin duda
de velar al sentenciado
sin parcialidad ninguna.

Siendo que tocó quedar solo
a Bell allí cuidando
mientras Bob se fué a cenar
pues su hora se le iba llegando
y el Bill no estando dormido
logra la oportunidad
y pronto está decidido
de tomar su libertad.

Pues la esposas tenía,
en una las dos,
que con toda su energia
le dió un golpe tan feroz,
que Bell cayó en sangre fría
sin aclamar a su Dios.
Con la pistola de Bell
con un balaso acabó.
de concluir el acto cruel
y luego se preparó.

Bob cuando cenando estaba
oyó un tiro resonar
Sus pasos apresuraba
sin acabar de cenar.
De la raya no pasó
donde había de quedar
pues alli el Bill lo mató
sin acabar de llegar.

And thus the aforementioned
    "Bilito"
added to his already long list,
two of the most valued citizens,
    now gone to their rest.
With his own hand cruel and
    bitter
and armed with a Winchester,
"Bilito" takes his pistol and
    munitions
making requisition
that a horse they should saddle
with sufficient precision.
And so, in the barn,
a swift steed he mounts
and with a wicked smile
he bids all, Good-bye.

To some unknown parts
went the famous "Bilito"
and traveling cautiously
he sees himself freed.
Upon hearing of the horrible act
the whole country is up in arms
    and
decrees that Pat Garrett, the
    famous
should go out in search of the
    rascal
with determination
firm and without wavering
Pat leaves with precision
his friends to avenge.

The news spread about
that around the Fort
"Bilito" was hiding
and that without doubt he was
    there.
Two men Pat Garrett took
from Lincoln when he left,

Y así el Bilito
añadió a su lista larga
a dos de los mas apreciados
con su mano cruel y amarga.
Con su Winchester armado,
su pistola y munición
sale el Bilito malvado
haciendo requesición—
que el caballo le ensillaron
con bastante precision.
Y así en la caballeriza
monta el caballo veloz
y con criminal sonrisa
les dice a todos—adiós.

A partes desconocidas
se fué el Bilito mentado
y andando a las escondidas
se ve ahora libertado.
Al oirse el acto horroroso
fué el grito del Pueblo alzado
que Pat Garrett, el famoso,
saliera en pos del malvado
Con su determinación
tan firme y sin quebrantar
sale Pat con precisión
sus amigos a vengar.

Razón se había tenido
que junto al Bosque se hallaba
el Bilito escondido
Y que allí sin duda estaba.
Dos hombres Pat Garrett toma
de Lincoln cuando salió

and without further hesitation
for the Fort departed.

He hides himself discretely
before entering the place.
When the people were asleep
Pat decides to enter
with Pedro Maxwell Pat went to
    speak
as soon as he arrived,
And to Pedro's room without
    hesitating
he swiftly made his way.

Pat without reservations tells
Señor Maxwell his intentions.
giving the reason for his visit
at that hour, to his room.
The two could not have been
    talking
for more than a quarter of an hour
when at that unheard of moment
they saw a man entering.
As Pat had left his companions
in the portal standing
they were the first to see
Bill, the hounded.

Bill approached the bed
with sufficient precaution.
He asks Pedro in a soft voice,
    —Those outside, who are they?
Then Pat give indications
of drawing out his pistol
which caused Bill to step back
on account of the movement.

"Bilito" recoiling,
with his revolver aimed, and
kept asking Pat
    —Who is it? but he does not
    fire.

sin tener ninguna broma
al Fuerte se dirijió.

Se oculta discretamente
antes de entrar al lugar.
Cuando ya duerme la gente
determina Pat entrar.
con Pedro Maxwell fué a hablar
el Pat luego que llege
y al cuarto sin titubear
de Pedro se dirigió.

Pat con poco resquisito
da al senor Maxwell su intento.
La causa de su visita
aquella hora a su aposento
No estarir un cuarto de hora
ellos los dos platicando
cuando a aquella insudita hora
ven un hombre al cuarto entrado.
Como que Pat al entrar
dejo a sus dos compañeros
parados en el portal
ellos ven al perseguido Bil,
    primero.

El "Bil" se acercó a la cama
con bastante precaución,
pregunta a Pedro en voz sana
    —Los de afuera ¿quienes son?
Luego da trazas de sacar
Pat su pistola al momento,
lo que hizo al Bil recular
a causa del moviminto.

El Bilito reculando
con su pistola asestada
a Pat sigue preguntando
    —¿Quién es? pero no dispara.

This gave Pat a chance
to make sure of his aim
and without further delay
he fired the fatal shot.
Instantly Bill fell, shot through the
        heart
and without complaining he died
a rare thing in a boaster.

It is necessary to state
that Bill came in his stocking feet.
Meat he had come to fetch
from don Pedro, should he have it.
When into the room, Bill entered
Pat unaware was sitting
Immediately he recognized him
and appeared a little frightened.

With the death of Bilito
this village finds itself relieved
since they were constantly afraid
of finding themselves surrounded.
This episode so famous
to which Pat added so much
        glamour
deserves to be well rewarded
because of the action, so arrogant.

And now this puts an end to
        "Bilicito"
after his very short life
He committed so many crimes,
his death was necessarily
        applauded.
And so "Bilito" followed
his very good companions
Tom Folliard and Charley Bowdre,
but it could not be otherwise!

        End

Esto le dió a Pat lugar
de apuntar bien su arma
Le deja ir el fatal tiro
al instante el Bill cayó
traspasado el corazón
y sin quejarse murió
cosa rara en un blasón.

Es preciso mencionar
que el Bil en medias venía.
Carne venía a quitar
a don Pedro si tenía.
Cuando al cuarto el Bil entró
el Pat estaba sentado
De una vez lo conoció
y se vió un poco asustado.

Con la muerte del Bilito
se halla este pueblo aliviado
pues les daba temoricito
hallarse por él, rodeado.
Esta acción tan afamada
que hizo Pat tan importante
merece ser bien premiada
por su acción tan arrogante.

Ya concluyó el "Bilecito"
despues de tan corta vida
Cometió tanto delito
que su muerte fué aplaudida.
Y así siguio "Bilito"
a sus compañeros buenos,
Tom Folliard y Charley Bowdre
pues no se podía menos.

Fin[54]

►12◄

THE KID DID NOT DIE

LIKE OTHER LEGENDARY HEROES, Billy the Kid was popularly thought to have lived far longer than his alleged death date of July 14, 1881. In fact, as Stephen Tatum notes, "Billy the Kid is not legally dead because no original copy of the coroner's jury inquest has been filed in New Mexico."[55]

MR. POE

COLLECTED BY D. D. SHARP, 1938

The following was gleaned from an interview with Mr. Poe who was well acquainted with Billy the Kid and for a while rode the range with him for the McSween outfit. Mr. Poe showed me a pair of handcuffs that Billy had worn which were given to him by Pat Garrett. He said that the leg irons were in possession of a Mr. Tittsworth of Capitan, New Mexico. These leg irons were cut by the jail cook with an ax while Billy the Kid held a gun on him. The handcuffs were different than any I have ever seen, heavy affairs, capable of inflicting a knockout blow if properly laid on. Mr. Poe tells a story of Billy's escape. Billy was playing Bucking Monte with a man named Bell who (Bell) had loosened the handcuffs a little to make it easier on the Kid. These handcuffs have three notches to draw the wrist bands smaller or make them larger. Billy dropped a card to the floor as though by accident, and when Bell reached down to get the card the Kid grabbed his gun and told him not to move. Mr. Poe says Billy liked Bell but when he got excited and ran there was nothing for the Kid to do but kill him or be killed himself.

Mr. Poe first met Billy the Kid in 1879 or 1880 or thereabouts when he (Poe) was trail driving cattle from Coleman County, Texas,

87

to Mack Sween's ranch near Lincoln, New Mexico. Billy the Kid was riding for McSween at the time and when Mr. Poe and his riders approached McSween's range, Billy, Bill Kellum (Cherokee Bill), Frank Coe, and a rider named Googin were sent by McSween to escort the cattle in. There had been some trouble between McSween's outfit and that of a cattleman named Murphy.

Mr. Poe says that he doubts very much if Pat Garrett really killed Billy the Kid. For one thing he says that Frank Coe told him some six or eight years ago that he (Coe) could saddle his horse at sunrise at his ranch on the Ruidoso near the resort there, and eat supper with Kid at sundown. Another thing that leads him to believe that the Kid was not killed then is the story that Pat Garrett told of the killing. Mr. Poe's cousin, John Poe, was deputy sheriff under Pat Garrett. John Poe and a cattle association man, Mr. Poe says, were sitting outside Pete Maxwell's room when Billy the Kid came along with a butcher knife to cut a piece of meat. They had just butchered a beef. Poe said he ran right into them and the Kid pulled his pistol and said, "Quien es? Quien es?" for he couldn't see them very well. Poe answered, "Don't get skeered my man. Don't get skeered, we're friends," and Billy demanded again "Quien es? Quien es?" as he backed into the room where Maxwell and Pat Garrett was on the bed and shot the Kid as he came into the door. Mr. Poe says a man like the kid with a price on his life would never have asked, "Quien es?" but would have killed the two without question. Another thing he states is that nobody was allowed to see the remains of the man that was shot except Pete Maxwell and family, Pat Garrett, John Poe, McKine, and an old Mexican woman, and a woman who was supposed to have been and may have been Billy's mother, who had gotten there very miraculously since it should have taken some six days to get word to her at Silver City and get her back again.

He mentions Perry Carney who was the right hand of Pat Coglin, cattle king, who lived at Tularosa and the 'little Irishman' worked for him, and received the stolen cattle the Kid brought.

"Perry Carney told me and two Mexicans told me the Kid positively was not killed. Carney told me the Kid came over and got a saddle after Pat Garrett was supposed to have killed him. He shot in the dark, missed him the second time clear. If he had missed him the first he'd a been a dead man, if it was the Kid." At this point I asked Mr. Poe why Billy started on a crime career and his reply:

"We lived right there in Silver City. He went with his mother downtown there one day and a blacksmith kinder insulted his mother. The Kid was only about 13 or 14 years old then, and the Kid got kinder excited and threw rocks at him. A fellow by the name, I can't recall his name, jumped up and defended the Kid, you know. One night the Kid was in a saloon there in Silver City and this friend that had taken up for him and knocked the blacksmith down, got into trouble himself. This blacksmith grabbed a chair. This Martin, or some name like that, ran by behind him (the Kid's friend) fixing to hit him with the chair. Then the Kid stabbed him. That is what started it.

"He went on down to Tucson, got to working for a cow ranch, chased around there for a good while, then him and another fellow started back west. They were afoot and they met three Indians. These Indians had been trapping and they were loaded with fur and had four good horses. The Kid has his sixshooter—he always had that. Killed the three of them and took their horses and fur. At that time that was not so bad, the Indians were on the warpath.

"He went on down into Mexico and got tangled up there and rode on to Old Mesilla just below Las Cruces. Got with the other fellows there, you know, doing a little stealing. Anyway they had to get back to Mexico to scatter 'em. While he was gone the others went over to the Pecos there beyond Lincoln County, and the Kid made his way there and was into it there in the killing of Tungsten. Tungsten was a great friend of his. Billy was working for him. Tungsten was killed by a sheriff's posse while he was unarmed, sent by Sheriff John Brady, who was killed by Billy the Kid. Morton and Baker was killed there. I saw him kill them. That was one of the times I saw the Kid in action."[56]

Unidentified New Deal Public Works of Art painting showing Pete Maxwell's old house at Fort Sumner (upper left) with a railroad train on a bridge with a banner reading "1907" in the background (upper right). Recognizable figures include (counterclockwise from left): two standing men—Pete Maxwell (right), Lucien B. Maxwell (left), an unidentified seated man, Deluvina Maxwell, the Kid's horse, Billy the Kid, a recumbent Tom O'Folliard, Charles Bowdre, Mrs. Charles Bowdre,

and three standing men, probably Lincoln County sheriffs Jim Brent (left), John William Poe (center), and Pat Garrett (right). The portraits are of an unidentified woman—possibly Paulita Maxwell or Celsa Gutierrez, both romantically linked with the Kid—and Pat Garrett. (The portraits may also depict Susan and Alexander A. McSween.) WPA Collection, School of American Research, No. 5365, New Mexico State Records Center & Archives, Santa Fe.

JOSE GARCIA Y TRUJILLO OF ALBUQUERQUE
COLLECTED BY JANET SMITH, 1936

Jose Garcia y Trujillo doesn't believe that Billy the Kid was ever shot. He feels sure he got away to South America. He wouldn't be surprised if he is alive somewhere today, an old man with many memories and a quick mind, like himself. When I showed him a book by the man who killed Billy the Kid [Pat Garrett, *The Authentic Life of Billy, the Kid, Noted Desperado of the Southwest*, 1882], he was unconvinced.

"No, *señora*," and he shook his forefinger back and forth before his face. "You think Billy the Keed let himself be shot in the dark like that? No *señora*—Billy the Keed—never. I see Billy the Keed with these eyes. Many times, with these eyes. That Billy, *tenia un agilesa in su mente—in su mente aquí*." He pointed to his forehead.

Mr. Garcia could speak but little English, and I knew almost no Spanish, but I understood that he meant that Billy the Kid had an extraordinary quickness of mind. Again he pointed to his forehead and then with a quick motion to the sky. "*Un función eléctrica*," he said. Something that worked like lightning.

When I stopped to see Mr. Garcia he was sitting on the ground under the cottonwood tree that shades the cracked adobe walls of his long narrow house. His hat was pulled down over his eyes and he seemed to be sleeping. As I stopped the motor of my car, however, he raised his head and pushed back his hat with one motion. He squinted at me a minute, then pulled himself to his feet.

"*Comó se va, Señora?*" Mr. Garcia placed the one chair in the shade for me. He found a box behind a heap of wagon wheels and car fenders and sat down beside me. He squinted his long blue eyes and asked in Spanish, "What's new?"

I patted the black kitten stretched on a bench at my elbow. Beside it perched a cock and two hens. Two little brown dogs nosed at my shoes, and a big shaggy fellow laid his head against my arm. The flies buzzed.

A thin, dark old woman stepped over the little goat sleeping just inside the doorway of the house, its head resting on the doorstep. She gathered up some green chili from a table in the yard, giving me an intent look as she stood there, and went back into the house without saying a word.

Mr. Garcia asked me again, "What's new? You bring me those history books of Billy the Keed?"

I showed him the picture of Pat Garrett who shot Billy the Kid. "I don't want to dispute against you, Señora, but in my mind which is the picture of my soul, I know it is not true. Maybe Pat Garrett, he give Billy the Keed money to go to South America and write that story for the looks. Maybe he kill somebody else in Billy's place. Everybody like Billy the Keed—*su vista penetrava al corazón de toda la gente*—his face went to everybody's heart."

Mrs. Garcia came out again and sat on a bench beside her husband. Her skin looked dark and deeply wrinkled under the white towel she had wrapped about her head. She rolled a brown paper cigarette from some loose tobacco in a tin box. As her husband talked she listened intently, puffing on her cigarette. From time to time she would nod her head at me, her eyes dark and somber.

"What did Billy the Kid look like?" I asked.

"*Chopito*—a short man, but wide in shoulders and strong. His forehead was big. His eyes were blue. He wore Indian shoes with beads on his feet. His clothes—*muy desorallado*—"

"*Desorallado?*" I asked.

"Like yours," he said, pointing to my blue denim skirt and shirt. "Any old way.

"*Muy generoso hombre*, Billy the Keed—a very generous man. All the Mexican people, they like him. He give money, horses, drinks—what he have. To whom was good to Billy the Keed he was good to them. *Siempre muy caballero, muy señor*—always very polite, very much of a gentleman. Once lots of mens, they go together after Billy the Keed to shoot him. They pay us—we go— sure. But we don't want to shoot Billy. We always be glad he too smart for us."

In broken English mixed with Spanish phrases Mr. Garcia told

me how he went in a posse of thirty-five or more men to capture
Billy the Kid. He didn't know the sheriff's name, but the description sounded like Pat Garrett himself—*"muy, muy alto,"* very, very
tall and Pat Garrett was six feet four and a half. Jose Garcia was
working at the time as sheepherder on the ranch of Jacobo Yrissari
about ninety miles southeast of Albuquerque. The tall sheriff came
by one day with a band of men and offered him five dollars a day
and food for himself and his horse to join the posse in search of
Billy the Kid. He said he didn't think there was any danger of their
getting Billy and five dollars was a lot of money. The plan was to
surround the Maxwell Ranch on the Pecos River where Billy the Kid
was known to spend much time.

This ranch belonged to Lucien Maxwell. *"Un muy grande
hombre, un millonario,"* said Jose Garcia.

Lucien Maxwell was indeed one of the most striking figures of
the early mountain frontier. Every trader and plainsman in the
Rocky Mountain region knew him. He came to New Mexico from
Illinois when the country was still a part of Old Mexico. There he
married Luz Beaubien, daughter of a French Canadian, Charles
Hipolite Trotier, Sieur de Beaubien, and a Spanish woman. With
Guadalupe Miranda, Beaubien had received from the Mexican
government during the administration of Governor Manuel Armijo
[1841] a huge grant of land as a reward for pioneer services.
Beaubien bought Miranda's share and at Beaubien's death Lucien
Maxwell, his son-in-law, purchased all the land from the heirs and
became sole owner of more than a million acres. He made huge
sums of money selling sheep, cattle and grain to the government
and built a great house at Cimarron [ca. 1857].

There he lived in as much magnificence as the times and the
country could afford. His guests included cattle kings, governors,
army officers and later, when he moved to the ranch near Fort Sumner [1870], Billy the Kid. Nearly every day his table was set for more
than two dozen, and it is reputed that they ate on plates of silver
and drank from goblets of gold. Jose Garcia said he didn't know
anything about that for he had never been inside of the house, but
he thought it quite likely. He had been by the place at Cimarron
several times when he was working for some people by the name

of Martinez who had a ranch north of Las Vegas.

The Maxwell house was *"una grande mansión,"* but it was to the Maxwell house on the Pecos near Fort Sumner that he went in search of Billy the Kid. Maxwell retired to his place at Fort Sumner after losing much of his wealth. His son Pete later became the richest sheep man in that part of the country. It was Pete who was a friend of Billy. Jose Garcia said he and the other men surrounded the house for two weeks but they never got so much as a glimpse of Billy the Kid.

Mr. Garcia said he knew a good friend of Billy the Kid, Jose Chavez y Chavez. When he was herding sheep on the Yrissari Ranch, which was not far from Santa Rosa on the Pecos River, Jose Chavez y Chavez was sheep herder on a nearby ranch. One day the two of them were sitting under a tree smoking when a pack train on the way to Arizona came along on the other side of the Pecos. Just opposite the tree where the two sheepherders were sitting they tried to ford the stream, but the water was swift and the horses floundered. Jose Garcia and Jose Chavez pulled off their clothes, jumped in and guided the horses to the bank. After the pack train went on Jose Chavez showed Mr. Garcia the twenty-one bullet scars on his body. "He had an innocent face—didn't look as though he could break a dish, but he was bad with a gun. *Que hombre!"*

"Did they try to get Jose Chavez to go with the posse after Billy?" I asked.

"Jose Chavez y Chavez," he corrected me. "No, *señora*, he had left the country at that time."

According to Walter Noble Burns, who wrote *The Saga of Billy the Kid* [Garden City, New York: Doubleday, Page & Company, 1926], it was this Jose Chavez y Chavez who was responsible for the friendship between Billy the Kid and the wealthy Maxwells. Billy the Kid had ridden over to Fort Sumner from Lincoln with several of his men, among whom was Jose Chavez y Chavez. The fiance of one of the Maxwell girls was drunk and met Jose Chavez y Chavez on the street back of the Maxwell house. The two men quarrelled and Jose Chavez pulled his gun. Mrs. Maxwell ran out of the house and tried to pull her future son-in-law away, begging Chavez not to shoot him as he was drunk and didn't know what he was doing. Chavez replied that drunk or sober he was going to kill him, and he was going to do it immediately. Just then a young man walked rapidly across the road, touched his sombrero to Mrs. Maxwell, said something in Spanish to Chavez and led him away. It was the Kid. From that time until his death he made Fort Sumner his headquarters and was a frequent visitor at the Maxwell home. It was in Pete Maxwell's room that Pat Garrett shot him.

Mr. Garcia asked me if there were any books in Spanish about Billy the Kid. "My wife," he said, "she taught me to read. I didn't know the letters when I married her. She didn't know the words but she knew the letters and she taught me. I taught myself how the words went, but I never could teach her how to read, *ni con cariños ni estímos*—neither by coaxing nor praising—she never could learn anything more than the letters."

Mrs. Garcia shook her head. "*Nunca, nunca, nunca,*" she said. Never had she been able to learn more than the letters.

I promised to look for a Spanish book about Billy the Kid. I sat for a minute longer watching some pigeons perched on a water barrel. They pecked at the water. The ripples reflected on their green and lavender breasts. The little goat came out of the house and sniffed the dirt around my chair.

As I rose to go Mr. Garcia stood up and took off his hat. "*Muchas felicidades y buena salud, Señora,*" he said with a little bow. Much happiness and good health to you.

Mrs. Garcia put out her hand. Her dark eyes were always somber. "*Adiós,*" she said, "*no se mas que decir Dios se irá con usted.*" Goodbye, I can only say God be with you.

"*Vuelva,*" they called after me as I drove away. "Come back."[57]

96

►13◄

RELICS OF BILLY THE KID

LEGENDS AND RUMORS ABOUT THE KID'S remains and his ghost circulated almost immediately after his death. Whether his grave is in Fort Sumner, Fort Stanton, Las Cruces, Old Mesilla, or even Santa Fe, whether his trigger finger or skull were ever displayed, whether his ghost haunted various locales, or whether he died in New Mexico at all have long been in dispute in popular tradition.[58]

CHARLIE FOOR, ADELINE WELBORN, BILLY ABREA, AND BILL LEATHERMON

COLLECTED BY J. VERNON SMITHSON, 1936

Two and one-half miles east of Fort Sumner on U.S. Highway 60, and six miles south on a graveled, all-weather country road is the grave of Billy the Kid.

One of the famous characters of the Southwest, Billy the Kid was credited with having killed over twenty-one men in his lifetime. A man for every year that he lived.

Billy the Kid made his headquarters in Fort Sumner the last years of his life and had many friends in the town.

He was killed July 14, 1881, in old Fort Sumner at the home of Lucian B. Maxwell, traces of which may still be seen to the west of the cemetery where Billy the Kid is buried.

In a little unkept cemetery, dotted with crosses of many unknown graves, Billy the Kid lies in company with his two pals, Tom O'Folliard and Charley Bowdre, who were killed a short time before Billy the Kid met his death at the hands of Pat Garrett, who was also responsible for the deaths of O'Folliard and Bowdre.

Enterprising citizens of Fort Sumner have erected a monument marking the graves of Billy the Kid, Tom O'Folliard, and Charley Bowdre; the three were buried side by side.

Lawless they might have been, they sleep in peace in this dreamy little cemetery where nothing disturbs the quiet but the soft gurgle of water in the nearby ditches and the cooing of doves to their mates. In such surroundings it is easy for the imagination to conjure back the days of Old Fort Sumner and Billy the Kid.[59]

FROM THE *LIBERTY BANNER*, LINCOLN, MAY 21, 1891

COPIED AND SUBMITTED BY EDITH L. CRAWFORD, 1937

Billy the Kid's Gun

Its Present Possessors Offer it as a World Fair Attraction Special to the St. Louis Republic.

Chicago, Ill., May 2, —A Missouri man who has an eye for business as well as for the beautiful, offers the World's Fair management a gem and makes his tender in the following letter:

I have a gun in my possession, a Winchester rifle, that was captured with Billy the Kid. He was an outlaw and figured in New Mexico. Very likely you have read his history. He was a robber, and murderer of the deepest dye. He was captured in Lincoln County New Mexico and was condemned to hang. The day before the execution he killed the 2 guards and made his escape and was finally captured by one Pat Garrett, the sheriff of Lincoln County. He was captured in Peat Maxwells on the Pecos River, New Mexico. Garrett killed him in the house. He was 21 years old and killed a man for every year he was old. Every time he killed a man he made a straight mark on the breech of his gun also his full name cut by own hand in print on the breech of his gun as they were killed with his gun. I was in New Mexico when he was captured and I made a purchase of the gun now if you would like to put this gun on exhi-

98

House in Lincoln, New Mexico, where Billy the Kid was held captive. The sign reads: "Billy the Kid carved his initials on door frame while prisoner here in 1876." Photo by Walter Wiggins. Courtesy Museum of New Mexico, Neg. No. 57308.

bition at the World's Fair let me know by return mail. This is no fine gun for it has seen hard service and been in rough hand and it is use to me. Yet if you wish for me to let you have it ile express it to you providing you send me a good shot gunn in return a muzzle loader i doo not care if it is a second hand just so it is a good gun. When I hear from you ile send Billy's gunn. And if you are not please with it express it back to me. If pleased express a good shot gun.

The World's Fair people considerately refuse to give the writer's name or address.[60]

MISS BILLY ABREA AND PETER ABREA

J. VERNON SMITHSON, 1936

Located on the outskirts of Fort Sumner, 12 miles from the business section of town, on U.S. Highway 60 east, is a little studio of relics and curios relating to the life of Billy the Kid, Old Fort Sumner, the Maxwell family and other associated characters.

From the room in which Billy the Kid met his death at the hands of Sheriff Pat Garrett is the bed in which Peter Maxwell was sleeping when both of these men called to see him and met in the darkness of his room. Tapestry, pitchers, candle-sticks, tables and other furnishings of the room, including the wash-stand which was pierced by Garret's second bullet gave one an intimate picture of the death of this famous character of the Southwest.

A picture of Lucian B. Maxwell, painted in his working clothes. The exact age of this picture is not known or the artist who painted it, but it is said that it was painted while Maxwell lived in the Cimarron country of New Mexico and was dated somewhere between 1840-1860.

Account books and ledgers kept by Lucian B. Maxwell dating back as far as 1850 showing accounts with Kit Carson and with the soldiers of Bosque Redondo Reservation and old Fort Sumner.

The first piano that was brought to New Mexico, given to his wife by Lucian B. Maxwell after his return from the gold rush of

Billy the Kid's horse (center) beside Armijo House, Albuquerque, New Mexico, ca. 1882 (see note 63). Photo by Ben Wittick. Courtesy Museum of New Mexico, Neg. No. 86863.

California in 1849. This piano is in a fair state of preservation and does credit to its manufactures Kindt and Mans of New York. There is an old chest which Maxwell brought with him in 1849.

This museum also contains many pictures of famed personalities of the Southwest, Maxwell family, Billy the Kid, Pat Garrett, Deluvina Maxwell and others. Many pictures relating to Lincoln County War and scenes where engagements took place between the Tunstall-McSween and the Murphy-Dolan factions. Many of these historic buildings have been destroyed and these pictures cannot be replaced. Also there are pictures of Juan Patron's store, the Montanies house and a picture of Ben Ellis' home where Billy the Kid met Governor Lew Wallace, when Wallace tried to get the Kid to stop his lawless ways and promised him immunity from his former enemies in the Lincoln County War.

A rifle said to have been given to Pete Maxwell by Billy the Kid is one of the earliest repeating rifles to be manufactured. The date of manufacturer is 1860 and it was made by the Spencer Repeating Rifle Co. of Boston. Other old guns and pistols are in this museum too.

A nominal fee of 25c is charged for viewing these relics so closely connected with the early history of this region. Well informed lecturers explain the connections and give an interesting discourse on the history of these relics.[61]

►14◄

N. HOWARD (JACK) THORP'S
VIEW FROM THE 1930s

COWBOY WRITER N. HOWARD (JACK) THORP'S rather jaundiced view of Billy the Kid was originally submitted to the Santa Fe office of the New Mexico Federal Writers' Project in 1937. In collaboration with Neil M. Clark, Thorp, who died in 1940, revised this manuscript for his account of Southwestern cowboy life, Pardner of the Wind, *posthumously published in 1941.*[62]

WILLIAM H. BONNEY, "BILLY THE KID"

SUBMITTED BY N. HOWARD THORP, 1937

William H. Bonney was born in New York City, November 23, 1859. In 1862, the family consisting of Father and Mother and two boys of whom Billy was the elder, emigrated to Coffeyville, Kansas. Soon after settling there, the Father died, and the Mother and two boys removed to Colorado, where she married a man named Antrim, who outlived the other members of the family. The family next moved to Santa Fe, New Mexico, where at eight years of age—according to Pat Garrett—he became adept at cards, "Some statement" what?

In 1868 when Billy was nine years of age, Antrim moved his family to Silver City in Grant County, New Mexico. At this time—according to old timers in Silver City—Billy got so mean Antrim not only could not keep him in school, but repeated whippings would not keep him out of the saloons. This wonderful affection which he was supposed to have towards his Mother, seems all drivel. Mrs. Antrim seems to have been a good woman, and tried to raise the Kid right, and if he had had any affection for her she could have controlled him, and kept him at school and at home.

At the age of twelve the historians claim Billy committed his first crime by stabbing a man in the back, but as no one seems to be able to identify this victim of the stabbing affray, or whether there really was any such occurrence we shall have to charge this episode to hearsay, so Billy cannot be given credit for it.

In Pat Garrett's book he states that it is impossible after our youthful projedy [sic] reached Arizona—where he went after one of Pa Antrim's spankings—to give any exact detail or dates as to what happened to him there. Garrett mentioned the fact, that after being a-foot for several days, he found his way to McKnight's Ranch where he and another kid, he had met on the road repaid McKnight's hospitality by stealing a pony, and the two boys thus mounted arrived at Ft Bowie, Arizona, this boy was nicknamed Alias.

Now a man cannot be proved guilty of murder, unless a corpse is produced.

Billy now claims that he and the Alias kid killed three Indians in order to rob them, but the corpses were never found, and don't you suppose when the three Indians were missed, their Apache brethren would have trailed these two green City kids up, and recovered the plunder?

Historians speak of the Kid's skill at cards, and how wonderful he was as a Monte dealer—mind you at twelve years of age—and how this skill kept the two boys, in luxuriant style—and as Garrett expresses it—gave them enviable prestige among the sporting fraternity of Arizona. Now regarding the horse race, he is supposed to have pulled off at San Simon, he may be given the benefit of the doubt, though it looks fishy.

Next the statement is made that Billy killed a blacksmith at Ft. Bowie, Arizona, but the murder is qualified by the statement that there is no record as to the date, and particulars of this crime, and Billy was always reticent in regard to this matter, and as we have only the Kid's statement, we will not give him credit for it.

Now regarding his trips into Mexico, the murders there he committed, and his wonderful skill at cards, and especially the killing of Don Jose Martínez, there is absolutely no evidence to support them, Billy had evidently been reading some dime thriller when he made up the story of his trip to Mexico. For the next five years, he seems to have been booted around considerable, and in 1876, when at the age of seventeen he again met his Silver City friend Jesse Evans.

The Kid's biographer now proceeds to state that the youthful pair made themselves well known, in western Texas, New Mexico, and the Rio Grande, by many deeds of daring crime, but fails to mention any crime which they committed. We want proof! So far, Billy has attained the age of seventeen, and the only crime he has committed was to steal a little pony from a friend, though Garrett on page 21 of his book, speaks of Billy's polite and cordial and gentlemanly bearing, let us hope so. Garrett also states that when Billy swore his oaths were expressed in the most elegant phraseology. Note page 23. The next thing that happens is a fight in which Billy and his partner whipped fourteen Indians and saved the wagon trains. Proof is wanted. Next when attempting to steal horses, from the Mescalero agency, he stated that he shot the bookkeeper Bernsteen, who attempted to stop him, this was on the fifth of August, 1878, only he didn't. A Mexican boy named Sanchez wanted to be called bad killed Bernsteen. Note page 113.

Concerning the man Grant it is true that Bonney killed him, but the evidence shows that Bonney had borrowed Grant's gun, and before returning it had twirled the cylinder so that when the hammer next came down it would strike a blank shell. The fact has frequently been emphasized in Garrett's book how square Bonney was with his friends. Well let's see. How about the eight hundred dollars he received from the sale of a bunch of Chisum cattle, he, Bowdre, and O'Foillard are said to have stolen? In settling up he gave Bowdre thirty dollars, O'Foillard a new pair of boots, and kept the rest. Note page 118. The Mexicans, who had helped steal the cattle got nothing, and Scurlock, and his family were scared out of the country, after Bonney had given him a fifty pound sack of flour which he got from Maxwell's store, and still owes for. "Gallant I say."

In 1830, when Bonney stole the horses from the Mescalero Apache Indians, he cheated his partners Billy Wilson, Mose

Dedrick, Pasqual Chavez, Eugenio Salazar, and a man named Mora out of most of the horses. Note Garrett's book page 127.

Now regarding the Tunstall affair, Morton, Baker, and McClosky were shot to death by Frank McNab, as stated by Burns in his saga of Billy the Kid. The Kid who left the Tunstall Ranch on the Rio Feliz and his boss Tunstall accompanied by Brewer, U.S. Marshall Robert A. Winderman, these all quit Tunstall when a posse following them commenced shooting, leaving Tunstall to be killed.

Regarding the fight which occurred in the town of Lincoln in which several were killed, the facts are as follows: Sheriff Brady, Dept'y Hindeman, Billy Mathews, and George Peppin started for the court-house, and passed in front of the McSwain, Tunstall store. On top of the roof of the McSwain house, protected by the pretil [portal?] lay the following men, Sheriff Brady, and dept'y Hindeman. As there were two men killed and ten shooting at them the chances are five to one that the Kid did not commit the murder. These are the names of the men who did the shooting: Winderman, McNab, Billy the Kid, Tom O'Foilliard, Charley Bowdre, Fred Waite, and two others.

Concerning the attack on Buckshot Roberts, at Blazers Mill, the Kid claimed he fired the shot which killed Roberts. But Roberts himself, after licking the posse, in a dying statement asserted that Bowdre had fired the fatal shot. Fourteen men attacked one crippled soldier, lots of glamor.

Concerning the killing of Billy's guards Bell and Ollinger, while he was locked up in the old court house in Lincoln, there is a vast difference of opinion as to the exact happening. Some say that O'Foilliard was hidden in the brush behind the court house. When Billy appeared with his guard Bell, he killed the latter, and when Ollinger upon hearing the shot, ran out into the yard O'Foilliard killed him also. However, as there is no absolute proof whether this version or that of Pat Garrett's is right, we will bow to the later version, and give Billy credit for these two killings, which together with the man Grant makes three in all.

I was not in Lincoln County during these days of fighting, but arrived in New Mexico so shortly afterwards that all the events were

The caption on this picture attached to Jack Thorp's Writers' Project manuscript reads: "Sirs: How did you happen to miss the tintype of Billy the Kid (William H. Bonney) appearing in the Dec. 27th Oregonian? *I am sending it along because it is supposed to be the only full-face portrait extant of this great desperado. It was discovered by Rodger DeLashmutt of Glencullen, Ore. in an old family album. Prof. J. Frank Dobie, University of Texas, and Jack Potter, Clayton, N. Mex. who knew Billy, say the tintype is authentic. WILLIAM P. GRAY Portland, Ore."*

fresh in people's mind. I was well acquainted with the following men who all were on the ground at the time of the Lincoln County trouble: Jim Brent, Mason, Pat Garrett, Jim Redman, "Woodland" Poe, Pat Coughlin, Mrs. McSwain "Mrs. Barber," and many others.

Of the several books relative to William Bonney which I have read, Pat Garrett's is by far the most authentic, so I am giving from his book the numbers and names of the men which we know positively Bonney killed. He certainly is the most tooted and over estimated killer the state has produced. Many a photograph has been fostered upon the public as a likeness of Bonney, but the only authentic one, is that appearing in Garrett's book. I have here a photo, which recently appeared in February 15th issue of this year of Life Magazine, with the following foot note. Prof. J. Frank Dobie and Jack Potter, who knew Billy say the tintype is authentic. As close as I can arrive at Mr. Dobie's age it seems to be fifty-one, and as Billy was killed in 1881, or fifty-five years ago, there must of been some mistake. Mr. John Potter, which the little article claims, knew Bonney and identifies the picture—according to his statement in Who's Who—said he came to New Mexico in 1882, a year after Bonney's death.

However, these are some of those things which are continually popping up, and which we will try to correct.[63]

AFTERWORD

Jeff Dykes

As the bibliographer of the Kid (*Billy the Kid: The Bibliography of a Legend*, University of New Mexico Press, Albuquerque, 1952) with research for a second volume in progress, I thought I had heard about all the tall tales, figments of the imagination, faulty recollections, and downright lies about him. Not so! The staff of the New Mexico Writers' Project interviewed many of the old-timers in Billy Country during the late thirties. Examples from these interviews, which are quoted below, clearly indicate that legends do not die—they just grow.

To be sure, not all the interviews contribute to the legend. The old-timers were almost evenly divided in their opinions of the Kid; the women and Spanish-Americans were primarily pro and the Anglo men mostly anti. Some of those interviewed frankly stated that what they knew about the Kid was hearsay, and it is apparent that some of them had read the Ash Upson-Pat Garrett book [*The Authentic Life of Billy the Kid, the Noted Desperado of the Southwest, Whose Deeds of Daring and Blood Made His Name a Terror in New Mexico, Arizona, & Northern Mexico, a Faithful and Interesting Narrative by Pat F. Garrett, Sheriff of Lincoln Co., N.M., by Whom He was Finally Hunted Down & Captured by Killing Him*, first published 1882 and reissued in 1954 with an introduction by Dykes for The Western Frontier Library of the University of Oklahoma Press]. They repeated some of the stories from the fertile mind of Ash that appeared in the first third of the book. Despite the eighth quote in the examples below, that this is "by far the most authentic" of the books about the Kid, that statement is true only for the last third of it. The first third includes so many false statements (blindly copied by so many writers and would-be historians) that the responsibility for starting the legend is firmly fixed.

I think you will enjoy the recollections of these old-timers. Do be kind. Having just celebrated my eighty-sixth birthday, I can assure you that *time does dull memory*!

So They Say!—Some Examples

1. "Billy's Father came to Georgetown and settled. There he died. Mr. Antrim was a mining man at Georgetown. Billy Bonney's mother married Mr. Antrim and the family moved to Silver City in 1870." —The Kid's father (Michael McCarty) was never in New Mexico so far as is known. The Antrims were married in Santa Fe on March 1, 1873, and arrived in Silver City later that year.

2. "He (Billy) got in with a band of rustlers at Apache Tejo in the part of the country where he was made a hardened character." —Billy went to Arizona after breaking jail at Silver City. He worked as a cowboy and teamster.

3. "I know by himself (Billy) since he left New York, where he arrived at Ft. Sumner for (as) long he stayed there. It was the year 1872 when he came to Ft. Sumner. . . . He came to Ft. Sumner at 12 years of age and died on the 22nd of June, 1882. . . . He killed 22 men, all Americans, except 5 Apaches that he killed 12 miles west of Roswell." —There is no specific information about the McCartys and Antrim in the year 1872. They left Wichita, Kansas, late in 1871, presumably for Denver, Colorado, and it is not likely that they were in Ft. Sumner. The Kid was killed on July 14, 1881, and he did not kill 22 men.

4. "George Kimbrall was elected Sheriff of the county. Obeying the Governor's orders he called out the militia having commissioned Sr. Patron as Captain and Billy the Kid was First Lieutenant. During that year—that of '79 things were comparatively quiet and Billy had a very uneventful life." —Billy was "on the dodge" during most of 1879.

5. "In the spring of 1877, I went to the hot springs located near Silver City. There were no accommodations at the springs at that time so I stayed in Silver City at a hotel run by Mrs. Antrim. While I was there she cried and told me of her young son. . . . At that time I never dreamed of this being Billy the Kid's mother as I knew him as William Bonney." —The Kid's mother died (TB) on September 16, 1874.

6. "Billy the Kid's mother did not tell me the reason for his leaving home the first time I met her (1877). A few years later I returned to Hudson Hot Springs and I went to see Mrs. Antrim, Billy's mother. She told me then that the reason her son had to

leave home was because he had killed a man for making insulting remarks about her. He left home that night and she never saw nor heard from him again." —She likely read the Upson-Garrett book and certainly did not have a conversation with Mrs. Antrim (see 5 above).

7. "Of the several books relative to William Bonney which I have read, Pat Garrett's is by far the most authentic. . . ." —See afterword text above.

8. "One of the bloodiest occurrences in Billy's career was the blowing out of a store belonging to a Fort Sumner resident. Billy's crowd stopped at this store for whiskey. The store keeper refused to open his door to the unruly gang. The affront angering them, the crowd retreated to a safe distance and began shooting at barrels of powder which they spied through the store window. The powder exploded, the store went up in a rush of flame, the storekeeper lost his life, and one of Billy's crowd was mortally injured." —A first appearance of this one—highly unlikely!

9. "John Cummings told me the first time he saw Billie the Kid was in Cochise. The Kid came into town and went to a saloon and said he was hunting work. The boy saw men gambling and was soon in the game—he was a stranger in the country, and as he seemed to have all the luck and was taking all of the money; one of the men made a nasty remark. The Kid drew his gun and killed two of the men around the table and injured another. He walked out of the saloon as he had just been in the place for a drink, and walked over to his horse as unconcerned, looked back, and then jumped on and rode away. . . . The boy left Cochise and was never seen there again." —Another first—also highly unlikely!

Editor's Note: The above quotations appear on the following pages: 1, p. 2; 2, p. 2; 3, pp. 36, 38; 4, p. 73; 5, pp. 9-10; 6, p. 11; 7, p. 107; 8, p. 40; 9, p. 14-15.

NOTES

Marta Weigle

The WPA Federal Writers' Project:

President Franklin D. Roosevelt established the Works Progress Administration (WPA) by Executive Order No. 7034 on May 6, 1935, to coordinate and implement work relief programs "to assume a maximum employment in all areas." Lea Rowland of Roswell administered the WPA in New Mexico. Federal Project Number One, the first of six white-collar work relief projects, was announced on August 2, 1935. It included the Federal Writers' Project (FWP), designed to employ writers, teachers, map draughtsmen, photographers, reporters, editors, journalists, librarians, and research workers. Ina Sizer Cassidy of Santa Fe was hired to direct the NMFWP on October 1, 1935. She was demoted in January 1939 and replaced by Aileen O'Bryan Nusbaum, who served from February 1 until August 31, 1939. At that time, the WPA was reorganized as the Work Projects Administration and the FWP became the Writers' Program. New Mexico's contribution to the FWP's major undertaking, the American Guide Series, *New Mexico: A Guide to the Colorful State* (New York: Hastings House, 1940), was completed under the reorganized Writers' Program. Refs.: Monty Noam Penkower, *The Federal Writers' Project: A Study in Government Patronage of the Arts* (Urbana: University of Illinois Press, 1977); Marta Weigle, *New Mexicans in Cameo and Camera: New Deal Documentation of Twentieth-Century Lives* (Albuquerque: University of New Mexico Press, 1985).

The Collectors:

Editorial offices for the NMFWP were located in Santa Fe, and the state was divided into four districts. Field writers throughout these districts conducted library and newspaper research, interviewed local residents, and made site visits to surrounding landmarks and communities. Biographical sketches of the collectors represented in this volume and known dates of their NMFWP employment (as indicated by dates of manuscripts submitted) follow. (The designation "Weigle, *New Mexicans*," refers to *New Mexicans in Cameo and Camera*, cited above.)

Crawford, Edith L.: Of Carrizozo. Mss. May 1937-July 1939.

Dean, William (Willie) Steele: No information except four mss. dated May 1938.

Lynn, Bright: A student at New Mexico Normal (now Highlands) University who was employed as a Senior Writer on the NMFWP, July 1938 to July 1939, during his junior year. Of Irish and Cherokee descent, from Oklahoma, Lynn was a brilliant student who aspired to be a writer. He began folklore work with Aurora Lucero White. Reportedly in debt and despondent after his wife's return to Oklahoma, Bright Lynn committed suicide in the summer of 1939. Ref.: Marta Weigle, ed., *Two Guadalupes: Hispanic Legends and Magic Tales from Northern New Mexico* (Santa Fe: Ancient City Press, 1987).

Ragsdale, Katherine: Of Artesia. Mss. May-December 1936. According to her May 18, 1936, NMFWP autobiography, Ragsdale was born in Bisbee, Arizona, on March 11, 1911. At various times her family lived in Cincinnati, Ohio, El Paso, Texas, Douglas and Nogales, Arizona, and Artesia, New Mexico, where she began her schooling at the age of seven and where she graduated from high school. Ragsdale later studied voice at the Cincinnati Conservatory of Music, worked in an Oklahoma City department store, and moved back to Artesia on December 20, 1934, working in an office and then part-time in a department store before joining the NMFWP in April 1936.

Raines, Lester B.: Of Las Vegas. Mss. March-August 1936. Born in Illinois on July 23, 1896, and educated at the University of Illinois, Carnegie Institute of Technology, Harvard, and Ohio State University, where he earned a doctorate. While chairman of the English and Speech Department at New Mexico Normal (now Highlands) University, Raines set up four annual New Mexico Round Tables on Southwestern Literature, 1933-36. Chiefly interested in play production, he founded and directed a dramatic group, the Koshares, Delight-Makers of New Mexico, in 1928, when he came to Las Vegas. Ref.: Lester B. Raines, ed., *More New Mexico Writers and Writings* (Las Vegas: New Mexico Normal University, English Department, 1935).

Redfield, Georgia B.: Of Roswell. Mss. December 1935-August 1939. According to her May 16, 1936, NMFWP autobiography, she was born in Louisiana and educated in New Orleans. She came to New Mexico in January 1893, accompanying her sister, Mrs. R. H. Parsons, who was on her way to join her husband, a storekeeper-hotel owner in Picacho. Redfield first met Sidney I. Redfield in 1894, when he owned and edited the *Roswell Register.* They were married in Louisiana in 1900 and settled permanently in Roswell after 1910, raising their son and daughter there. Mrs. Redfield contributed news, descriptive articles, and poems to numerous magazines and newspapers. In 1938 she was appointed historian of the Chaves County Archaeological and Historical Society and later that year began collecting biographies for the NMFWP for a project book to be entitled "Pioneer Builders of Roswell in the Sunshine State—New Mexico." Refs.: James D. Shinkle, *Reminiscences of Roswell Pioneers* (Roswell, New Mexico: Hall-Poorbaugh, 1966), pp. 186, 195-99; Weigle, *New Mexicans*, pp. 194-95.

Reich, (Mrs.) Betty: Of Deming. Mss. April 1936-July 1937.

Sharp, D(rury) D.: Of Albuquerque. Mss. January 1936-November 1938.

Smith (Kromer), Janet: Of 1216 East Central, Albuquerque. Mss. March 1936-March 1938. Apparently she married Tom Kromer (NMFWP, 1936-39) by early 1937, when she first signs her submissions as Janet Smith Kromer.

Smithson, J. Vernon: Of Clovis. Mss. February 1936-July 1937. According to his May 5, 1936, NMFWP autobiography, he was born near Carnegie, Oklahoma, on October 8, 1912. His family moved to Curry County, New Mexico, in 1914, and Smithson attended grade school in Grady before moving in 1926 to Clovis, where he finished high school in 1931. He then traveled through the western and southern states, working at miscellaneous jobs before returning to Clovis in 1934 to work for the *Evening-News Journal*. Ref.: Weigle, *New Mexicans*, p. 196.

Thorp, N. Howard (Jack) (1867-1940): Of Alameda. Mss. February 1936-August 1939, and briefly on the Writers' Program afterward. Born June 10, 1867, and raised in New York City and Newport, Thorp was educated at St. Paul's School in Concord, New Hampshire. His first western experiences were on his brother Charles's ranch near Stanton, Nebraska, and he later came West while in his teens due to his father losing his money. Thorp's first New Mexico employment was as superintendent of Enterprise Mining Company in Kingston. He ran his own cattle in the San Andres Mountains and then began working for Bar W. Ranch in Lincoln County. He published three books: *Songs of the Cowboys* in 1908, *Songs of the Cowboys* in 1921, and *Tales of the Chuck Wagon* in 1926. For much of his NMFWP time he was working on a juvenile book entitled "Cowland: A Story of New Mexico Ranch Life." Ref.: Neil M. Clark, "Introduction," in Thorp with idem, *Pardner of the Wind* (1941; rpt. Lincoln: University of Nebraska Press, 1977), pp. 13-20.

Totty, Frances E. (Mrs. W. C.): Of Silver City. Mss. May 1937-November 1938. At one point during her NMFWP employment she wrote from the hospital, where she was recovering from being stabbed by her husband, whom she was suing for divorce. Ref.: Weigle, *New Mexicans*, p. 197.

White (Lea), Aurora Lucero (1894-1963): Of Las Vegas and Santa Fe. Employed on the NMFWP, August 1936-September 1937, White spent much of her time editing and translating folklore she herself had collected in San Miguel County before moving to Santa Fe in 1934. She studied at the University of Southern California before returning to finish an M.A. in Spanish literature and language at New Mexico Normal University in 1932. According to her NMFWP biography of August 9, 1937, she was "a daughter of Don Antonio Lucero, late Secretary of the State of New Mexico, a brilliant scholar, linguist, editor, and Professor of Spanish, [and] was born in Las Vegas, New Mexico. Don Antonio Lucero was a descendant of Antonio de Godoy, a Spanish Captain of New Mexico in 1650. Mrs. White's mother, Juliana Romero, was a descendant of Juan Romero de Roblero, who came to New Mexico from Spain. Mrs. White has taught Spanish, was Assistant County Superintendent of Schools of San Miguel County, and an Assistant in the State Department of Education, at Santa Fe." Her books include: *Folk-Dances of the Spanish-Colonials of New Mexico* (Santa Fe: Examiner Publishing, 1940); *New Mexico Folklore—Coloquio de los Pastores* (Santa Fe: Santa Fe Press, 1940); *The Folklore of New Mexico*, Volume I (Santa Fe: Seton Village Press, 1941); *Los Hispanos* (Denver: Sage Books, 1947); *Literary Folklore of the Hispanic*

Southwest (San Antonio, Texas: Naylor, 1953); *Juan Bobo, adapted from the Spanish Folktale Bertolo* (New York: Vantage Press, 1962). Ref.: "Notes on the Contributors," *American Stuff: An Anthology of Prose & Verse by Members of the Federal Writers' Project* (New York: Viking Press, 1937), p. 300; Marta Weigle with Mary Powell, "From Alice Corbin's 'Lines Mumbled in Sleep' to Eufemia's Sopapillas: Women and the Federal Writers' Project in New Mexico," *New America*, vol. 4, no. 3 (1982), pp. 56-57.

The Manuscripts:

Manuscripts submitted by field writers were usually retyped with two or three carbon copies in district or Santa Fe editorial offices. The same piece may thus be found in several typed versions in various locations. I would like to acknowledge a 1979-81 National Endowment for the Humanities grant to myself and William Wroth, then of the Taylor Museum of the Colorado Springs Fine Arts Center, to investigate "Governmental Support of the Arts in New Mexico, 1933-1943," enabling me to examine and inventory Washington, D.C., and Santa Fe holdings. In the notes below, the NMFWP manuscripts reprinted in this volume are identified as fully as possible by giving title, word and page count, date of writing, date of receipt in the Santa Fe editorial office, and the location(s) of the documents. The following abbreviations are used:

A#: Works Progress Administration (WPA) Files at the New Mexico State Records Center and Archives (NMSRC), Santa Fe. The 268 folders (30 expandable files) have been indexed by archivist Louellen N. Martinez as of July 18, 1983.

BC: Number assigned in a preliminary compilation by Gilberto Benito Cordova, *Bibliography of Unpublished Materials Pertaining to Hispanic Culture in the New Mexico WPA Writers' Files* (Santa Fe: New Mexico State Department of Education, December 1972). Some NMSRC documents are filed by BC numbers.

H#: Materials at the History Library, Museum of New Mexico, Santa Fe, were originally filed by file cabinet, drawer, and folder numbers, and most remain so. A card catalogue for many of these documents was assembled in the 1970s, but it has not been updated.

LC: Ann Banks of the American Studies Center, Boston College, compiled a "Survey of Federal Writers' Project Manuscript Holdings in the Archive of Folk Song, Library of Congress," dated December 28, 1979, when the holdings were under the care of the Folksong Archive (now Archive of Folk Culture). Manuscripts are numbered by file and drawer, from 36.2 to 48.4, as they are below. These holdings are now in the Manuscript Division of the Library of Congress.

The Notes:

1. Jon Tuska, *Billy the Kid: A Handbook* (1983; rpt. Lincoln: University of Nebraska Press, 1986), 3-5. Henry McCarty's boyhood home in Silver City was "a simple, gabled log cabin which stood on the east side of Main Street just north of Broadway" and "was demolished in 1894, after serving for several years as a shoe repair shop." The jail from which McCarty escaped through the chimney was "a small structure in the side yard of the county office building on Hudson Street" (Susan Berry and Sharman Apt Russell, *Built to Last: An Architectural History of Silver City, New Mexico* [Santa Fe: New Mexico Historic Preservation Division for Silver City Museum Society, 1986], 18).

2. Mrs. Frances Totty, coll., from Louis Abraham of Silver City, "Billie the Kid," 648 wds., 2 pp., 23 November 1937 (H5-4-2#20; LC47.1). Silver City boasts two Abraham blocks of storefronts—at 100-108 North Texas, built in 1906, and at 107 North Bullard, built in 1916, for Louis and Hyman Abraham, whose father David had opened a merchandise store in 1871 (Berry and Russell, *Built to Last*, 11, 59, 92, 98). In reminiscences for the *Silver City Enterprise* of 3 January 1902, Sheriff Harvey Whitehill recalled that the briefly jailed, young Billy the Kid "had one peculiar characteristic that to an experienced man-hunter would have marked him immediately as a bad man and that was his dancing eyes. They were never at rest, but continually shifted and roved much like his own rebellious nature" (quoted in ibid., 18).

3. Mrs. Frances Totty, coll., from the "wife of Mr. Louis Abraham" of Silver City, "Billie the Kid," 150 wds., 1 p., 2 November 1937 (H5-4-2#1, LC47.1).

4. Betty Reich, coll., "Indian Tales" and "Early Life of Billy the Kid," 391 wds., 2 pp., 2 April 1937 (H5-4-2#71; H5-4-2#21; LC47.1). Reich notes: "This information was given me by a long time resident of Silver City who asked me not to use his name."

5. Mrs. W. C. Totty, coll., from Dick Clark, "Billy the Kid," 670 wds., 2 pp., 15 November 1937 (H5-4-2#12). The Silver City cemetery occupied two blocks bounded by Tenth, West, Santa Rita, and Twelfth streets (Berry and Russell, *Built to Last*, 23).

6. Frances E. Totty, coll., from R. Athon of Silver City, "Billie the Kid," 400 wds., 1 p., 30 March 1938, rec. 5 April (H5-4-2#70; LC47.1). A photo of the Southern Hotel, ca. 1875, appears in Berry and Russell, ibid., 12.

7. Edith L. Crawford, coll., from Paul Mayer, age 82, of Carrizozo, "Reminiscences of Billy the Kid," 87 wds., 1 p., 20 December 1937 (H5-4-2#47; H5-4-2#24-B; LC47.1).

8. Edith L. Crawford, coll., from Dr. M. G. Paden, "age about 85," of Carrizozo, "Reminiscences of Billy the Kid," 210 wds., 1 p., 20 December 1937 (H5-4-2#46; H5-4-2#25; LC47.1).

9. Edith L. Crawford, coll., from Mrs. A. E. Lesnett, age 82, of Carrizozo, part of "Reminiscences," note 8. In 1868 Richard Hudson established a farm south of Pinos Altos at San Vicente Cienega and in June 1870 he participated in

116

the meeting to rename San Vicente as Silver City. He built the Hudson Hot Springs Hotel in 1872—"hacienda-style around a courtyard, [a] gable-roofed adobe...wrapped with ornate frame verandas," and it burned in 1890. (Barry and Russell, *Built to Last*, 9, 10, 37)

10. First paragraphs of Edith L. Crawford, coll., from Mrs. A. E. Lesnett, age 82, of Carrizozo, "Reminiscences of Billy the Kid," 1682 wds., 5 pp., 31 October 1937 (H5-4-2#42; LC47.1).

11. Edith L. Crawford, coll., from Mrs. Annie E. Lesnett, age 82, of Carrizozo, "Billy the Kid Story," 267 wds., 1 p., 1 June 1937 (H5-4-2#28; LC47.1).

12. Edith L. Crawford, coll., from Mrs. A. E. Lesnett, age 82, of Carrizozo, "Billy the Kid Story," 245 wds., 1 p., 22 November 1937 (H5-4-2#36; LC47.1). A further part of Mrs. Lesnett's account of her life and Billy the Kid's was published by Ann Banks in *First Person America* (New York: Alfred A. Knopf, 1980), 23-26.

13. Tuska, *Kid Handbook*, 6-7.

14. Frances E. Totty, coll., from Jim Blair of Santa Rita, Ed. Moulton's son-in-law, "Billie the Kid," 250 wds., 1 p., 10 December 1937 (H5-4-2#13; H5-4-2#43; LC47.1).

15. Frances Totty, coll., from Otho Allen, age 54, of Deming, "Early Days in the Southwest, By Otho Allen, Billy the Kid," 4 pp., 25 February 1938 (H5-4-2#67; LC47.1).

16. Tuska, *Kid Handbook*, 13, 16, 18-31; Robert M. Utley, *Four Fighters of Lincoln County* (Albuquerque: University of New Mexico Press, 1986), 7-13.

17. Edith L. Crawford, coll., from Robert Brady, age 71, of Hondo, "Billy the Kid Story," 1568 wds., 4 pp., 20 June 1938 (H5-4-2#34; H5-4-2#9; LC47.1). According to the 1940 New Mexico guide, assembled from NMFWP materials, the three-story El Torreon, with "caretaker next door west; 10c customary" was "built by early settlers in 1852 for protection against Indian raids" and "restored by the Chaves County Historical Society of Roswell in 1935" (Workers of the Writers' Program, WPA in New Mexico, *New Mexico: A Guide to the Colorful State* [New York: Hastings House, 1940], 385).

18. Edith L. Crawford, coll., from Gorgonio Wilson, age 66, of Roswell, "Billy the Kid Story," 361 wds., 2 pp., 14 February 1938 (H5-4-2#40). According to Robert Utley, Lincoln's John B. Wilson, also known as Green or Squire, was "a dull-witted, barely literate old man who presided as justice of the peace of the county's Precinct No. 1" (*Four Fighters*, 9).

20. Georgia B. Redfield, coll., from Mrs. J. P. Church, Vice-president of the Chaves County Archaeological and Historical Society, of 210 South Kentucky, Roswell, "Outlaw Shooting in Old Lincoln, Lincoln County, New Mex.," 500 wds., 2 pp., 22 January 1937 (H5-4-2#8; LC47.1). Governor Lew Wallace met privately with Billy the Kid at Squire Wilson's on a Monday night between March 15 and March 19, 1879 (Tuska, *Kid Handbook*, 66). Amelia Bolton Church helped raise the money to preserve El Torreon in Lincoln, where "as a little girl [she] witnessed the killing of Bell and Olinger.... Mrs. Church always had an

interest in the history of Lincoln County. She knew the early West as did few other women. She was the mother of Mrs. Langford Keith and Mrs. Sophia Ochampaugh, both of whom live in Roswell" (Cecil Bonney, *Looking Over My Shoulder: Seventy-five Years in the Pecos Valley* [Roswell, New Mexico: Hall-Poorbaugh Press, 1971], 61-62).

20. Tuska, *Kid Handbook*, 32-34. Utley calls the site Blazer's Mills (*Four Fighters*, 13, 15, 16, 27, 42).

21. Georgia B. Redfield, coll., "Battle at Blazer's Mill, Otero County," 800 wds., 3 pp., 22 April 1937 (H5-4-2#24; LC38.1). Redfield lists as her "Sources of Information": A. N. Blazer, son of Dr. Joseph Hoy Blazer, of Mescalero; Lucius Dills, 410 North Pennsylvania Avenue, Roswell; George Washington Coe, *Frontier Fighter: The Autobiography of George W. Coe Who Fought and Rode with Billy the Kid as related to Nan Hillary Harrison* (Boston: Houghton Mifflin, 1934; rpt. Albuquerque: Univeristy of New Mexico Press, 1951); and "the late W. L. Patterson—'Account of Lincoln County War' 1936."

22. Tuska, *Kid Handbook*, 37-38.

23. Edith L. Crawford, coll., from Donicino Molina, age 84, of Tularosa, "Billy the Kid Story," 155 wds., 1 p., n.d. (H5-4-2#30; LC47.1).

24. For a detailed account see Thomas J. Caperton, "The McSween House Site, Lincoln, New Mexico," in Nancy L. Fox, ed., *Prehistory and History in the Southwest*, Papers of the Archaeological Society of New Mexico: 11 (Santa Fe: Ancient City Press for the Society, 1985), 125-46.

25. Edith L. Crawford, coll., from Francisco Gomez, age 82, of Lincoln, "Billy the Kid Story," 215 wds., 1 p., 1 June 1937 (H5-4-2#29; LC47.1).

26. Edith L. Crawford, coll., from Francisco Gomez, age 85, of Lincoln, "What I Know About Billy the Kid," 318 wds., 1 p., 7 June 1937 (H5-4-2#26; LC47.1).

27. Edith L. Crawford, coll., from Manuel Aguilar, age 69, of Capitan, "Story of Billy the Kid," 262 wds., 1 p., 7 June 1937 (H5-4-2#26; LC47.1).

28. Edith L. Crawford, coll., from Mrs. Lorencita Miranda, age 78, of Lincoln, "Pioneer Story," 688 wds., 3 pp., 5 May 1939, rec. 6 May (A#210; LC47.1). Mrs. Miranda and others are discussed in Darlis A. Miller, "The Women of Lincoln County, 1860-1900," in *New Mexico Women: Intercultural Perspectives*, ed. Joan M. Jensen and Miller (Albuquerque: University of New Mexico Press, 1986), 169-200.

29. Lester B. Raines, coll., from Clara Fresquez of Lincoln," Billy the Kid By Clara Fresquez," 2 pp. 25 July 1936 (H5-4-2#3; LC47.1; LC47.2). In 1911 Teofilo Sisneros and Isidro Fresquez bought the McSween lot, which by then had a new house on it (Caperton, "McSween House Site," 141-42).

30. Kent Ladd Steckmesser, *The Western Hero in History and Legend* (Norman: University of Oklahoma Press, 1965), 95-102; Stephen Tatum, *Inventing Billy the Kid: Visions of the Outlaw in America, 1881-1981* (Albuquerque: University of New Mexico Press, 1982), 10-11. See also Lynda A. Sanchez, "Recuerdos de Billy the Kid," *New Mexico Magazine*, July 1981, pp. 16-19, 68, 70-71. It "is

based on the recollections of more than a dozen *viejos* (old ones), some of them interviewed by the author and some taken from interviews done by the Works Progress Administration (WPA) during the 1930s and preserved in the Museum of New Mexico History Library."

31. Letter to William Steele Dean from A. P. Anaya of Vaughn, 5 August 1926, 3 pp. (H5-4-2#65; LC47.1). See also note 43.

32. Lester Raines, coll., from Milnor Rudolph, "Billy the Kid," 2 pp., 21 March 1936 (H5-4-2#4; LC47.1).

33. L. Raines, coll., from Ismael Valdez, "About Billy the Kid By Ismael Valdez," 208 wds., 1 p., 3 August 1936 (H5-4-2#5; LC47.1).

34. Georgia B. Redfield, coll., from Berta Ballard Manning, "Pioneer Story: Child Friend of Billy the Kid, Little Berta Ballard," 255 wds., 2 pp., 3 February 1937 (H5-4-2#7; LC38.1).

35. Edith L. Crawford, coll., from José Montoya of Jicarilla, "Reminiscences of Billy the Kid," 376 wds., 1 p., 27 December 1937 (H5-4-2#41; LC47.1).

36. From Bright Lynn, coll., from Guadalupe Baca de Gallegos of Las Vegas, "This is a corrected copy of the BIOGRAPHY OF GUADALUPE LUPITA GALLEGOS which was sent in Nov. 8, 1938," 1450 wds., 6 pp., 30 December 1938, rec. 5 January 1939 (BC137; H5-5-51#7; LC47.1). On Sra. Gallegos see Marta Weigle, ed., *Two Guadalupes: Hispanic Legends and Magic Tales from Northern New Mexico* (Santa Fe: Ancient City Press, 1987). Sra. Gallegos (1853-1940) appears to have confused Billy the Kid's gang with Vicente Silva's. The latter's included Juan de Dios Lucero, whose son Sostenes became a noted criminal in Mora County (Tom McGrath, *Vicente Silva and His Forty Thieves* [Las Vegas, New Mexico, 1960], 6, 13-14).

37. Edith L. Crawford, coll., from Dr. M. G. Paden, age about 86, of Carrizozo, "Billy the Kid Story," 321 wds., 1 p., 22 November 1937 (H5-4-2#37; LC47.1).

38. Willie Dean, apparent coll., from Mrs. Carlota Brent, 601 Cooper, Silver City, and her son-in-law Mr. Shutz, "Lincoln County History," 2 pp., 23 May 1938 (H5-4-2#15; H5-4-2#72). See also note 49. Adolph Schutz, with Josh Brent joint owner of the Schutz-Brent building, 508-14 North Bullard, Silver City, is probably indicated (Berry and Russell, *Built to Last*, 101).

39. Tuska, *Kid Handbook*, 85-88.

40. Aurora Lucero-White, coll. and trans., "Campaña de los Bilitos / Campaign of the 'Bilitos,' " pp. 19-26, rewritten as 29-36, of "Romances and Corridos: Spanish Folkways of New Mexico," 26 October 1936 (BC338; H5-5-20#36; LC47.2). Diacriticals as in original. See also ms. of 18 August 1937 (H5-5-35#16). A version of the Spanish, "*Campaña de los Bilitos*," was published in Aurora Lucero-White Lea, *Literary Folklore of the Hispanic Southwest* (San Antonio, Texas: Naylor, 1953), 139-42.

41. Tuska, *Kid Handbook*, 221.

42. Katherine Ragsdale, coll., "Pioneer Story," 390 wds, 2 pp. 27 July 1936 (H5-4-2#2; LC47.1; LC47.2). For Barbara Jones's version see Eve Ball, *Ma'am Jones*

of the Pecos (Tucson: University of Arizona Press, 1969), 174-82.

43. From Edith L. Crawford, coll., from Paco Anaya of Vaughn, "Billy the Kid's Horse," n.d. (H5-4-2#35). See also note 31. This is the first two pages of an article apparently copied from *Western Livestock*, 2109 wds., 7 pp.

44. E. Crawford, coll., from Ladislado (Laiso) Salas, age 64, of Lincoln, "Story of Billy the Kid," 200 wds., 1 p., 17 May 1937 (H5-4-2#31; LC47.1).

45. Edith L. Crawford, coll., from Sam Farmer, age 68, of Carrizozo, "Pioneer Story," 690 wds., 2 pp., 25 July 1938 (H5-4-2#51; LC47.1).

46. Edith L. Crawford, coll., from Sam Farmer, age 67, of Carrizozo, "Reminiscences of Billy the Kid," 744 wds., 3 pp., 20 December 1937 (H5-4-2#39; LC47.1).

47. Tuska's "Bibliography of Historical Sources" lists a number of first-hand accounts, biographies, and general books (*Kid Handbook*, 136-38). Notable among the latter would be Maurice Garland Fulton, *History of the Lincoln County War*, ed. Robert N. Mullin (Tucson: University of Arizona Press, 1968); and William A. Keleher, *Violence in Lincoln County: 1869-1881* (Albuquerque: University of New Mexico Press, 1957).

48. Letter to William (Willie) Steele Dean from Frank B. Coe of Glencoe, 3 August 1926, 1 p. (H5-4-2#64; LC47.1). At the bottom of the page is the reference: "Footnote [351] of Twitchell's 'History of New Mexico' Vol. 2 page 423." The footnote is to Frank McNab's murder by "some thirty men of the Dolan and Riley faction" on a day when he was accompanied by Frank Coe and Abe Sanders. Sanders and McNab were shot, according to Twitchell: "Meanwhile Coe had put his horse to a gallop down the road, but was followed by a shower of bullets. When he had reached a point in the road fully twelve hundred yards below the camp, a ball from a buffalo hunter's rifle struck his horse, passing through its head and coming out at the eye. The horse turned a somersault in falling, while Coe escaped to the hills. He was there surrounded and taken prisoner and brought to Lincoln. The next day, while a fight was going on between the two factions, he escaped and joined his friends." (Ralph Emerson Twitchell, *Leading Facts of New Mexico History*, 2 vols. [Cedar Rapids, Iowa: Torch Press, 1911-12], 2, 423)

49. Edith L. Crawford, coll., from Francisco Trujillo, age 85, of San Patricio, "Billy the Kid," 3300 wds., 9 pp., 10 May 1937 (H5-4-2#21; LC47.1).

50. Frances E. Totty, coll., from Carolatta Baca Brent, born 17 January 1865, "Billie the Kid," 1000 wds., 3 pp., 1 January 1938, rec. 3 January (H5-4-2#11; LC47.1). See also note 38.

51. Frances E. Totty, coll., from Josh Brent, age 50?, of Silver City, "Early Days in Lincoln County," 700 wds., 2 pp., 26 May 1938 (H5-4-2#14; LC47.1). Emerson Hough (1857-1923) lived in White Oaks, 1883-85, working as a lawyer, reporter, and typesetter for the local newspaper, *The Golden Era*. Tuska discusses Hough's works on Billy the Kid in *Kid Handbook*, 123-25. Josh Brent owned property on North Bullard in Silver City (Berry and Russell, *Built to Last*, 101-2, 104).

52. Tuska, *Kid Handbook*, 101-4.

53. Frances E. Totty, coll., from John Allred, born March 1875, "Early Days in Lincoln County," 360 wds., 1 p., 13 July 1938 (H5-4-2#22).

54. Aurora Lucero-White, coll. and trans., "Muerte del Afamado Bilito / Death of the Famous 'Bilito,' " pp. 27-30, rewritten as 37-40, of "Romances and Corridos" (see note 40). Diacritical markings as in the original. See also ms. of 18 August 1937 (H5-5-35#17). A version of the Spanish, "*Muerte del Afamado Bilito*," was published in Lea, *Literary Folklore*, 142-44.

55. Tatum, *Inventing Billy*, 12; Sanchez, "Recuerdos de Billy," 68, 70-71.

56. D. D. Sharp, "Interview with Mr. Poe," 4 pp., 16 May 1938 (H5-4-2#60; LC47.1). On Mr. Poe's cousin, John William Poe (1850-1923), who followed Pat Garrett as Lincoln County sheriff, see Sophie A. Poe, *Buckboard Days*, ed. Eugene Cunningham (1936; rpt. Albuquerque: University of New Mexico Press, 1981).

57. Janet Smith, coll., from Jose Garcia y Trujillo of Albuquerque, "Pioneer Stories: Interview with Jose Garcia y Trujillo," 1800 wds., 7 pp. 26 August 1936 (A#212; LC47.1; LC47.2), as rpt. in Marta Weigle, *New Mexicans in Cameo and Camera: New Deal Documentation of Twentieth-Century Lives* (Albuquerque: Univeristy of New Mexico Press, 1985), 28-31.

58. Tatum, *Inventing Billy*, 12-13.

59. J. Vernon Smithson, coll., "Billy the Kid's Grave," 220 wds., 1 p. 21 April 1936, rec. 27 April (H5-4-2#6; LC38.3). Smithson lists as his "Sources of Information": "Personal observation of the writer—The Saga of Billy the Kid, Walter Noble Burns, Published by Double, Page & Co. Garden City, New York, 1927 [sic, 1926]. Personal interviews with Charlie Foor, Adeline Welborn, Billy Abrea, and Bill Leathermon."

60. Edith L. Crawford, coll., "Billy the Kid's Gun," copied from *Liberty Banner*, Lincoln, New Mexico, 21 May 1891, 377 wds., 1 p., 28 June 1937 (H5-4-2#10).

61. J. Vernon Smithson, coll., "Points of Interest," 460 wds., 2 pp., 11 May 1936 (H5-4-2#69; LC38.3). Smithson lists as his "Sources of Information": "Personal interviews with Miss Billy Abrea and Mr. Peter Abrea / Personal observation of the investigator."

62. "Billy ('The Kid') Bonney," in N. Howard (Jack) Thorp with Neil M. Clark, *Pardner of the Wind* (1941; rpt. Lincoln: University of Nebraska Press, 1977), 168-93.

63. N. Howard Thorp, coll., "William H. Bonney, 'Billy the Kid,' " 1750 wds., 6 pp., 25 March 1937 (H5-4-2#45; LC47.1). As for the authorities: Famous Texas folklorist and writer J. Frank Dobie (1888-1964) did not of course know Billy the Kid. In the 1880s Col. Jack Potter (1864-1948) worked for the New England Livestock Company and moved into its headquarters in the Fort Sumner buildings of the Lucien B. Maxwell estate in 1884. He lived there for nine years and became involved in the establishment's history. A hitch in the Maxwell estate sale came, as Potter notes: "when Pete Maxwell approached Lonny Horn stating that a horse in the remuda named 'Don' was the horse that Billy the Kid rode into Fort

121

Sumner from the Block Ranch in the Capitan Mountains, a full one-hundred-mile stretch, when he escaped after killing his two jailers. He also said that Billy had sent a check for his purchase with the instruction that the horse never be used on the ranch as he was wind-broken from the long hard ride. Pete Maxwell added seriously that if he sold this particular horse with the other livestock 'Billy, dead these three years, would rise up in his grave and curse me.' " Potter rode Old Don only around camp, and the horse died six years later, around 1890. (Jean M. Burroughs, *On the Trail: The Life and Tales of "Lead Steer" Potter*, with original stories by Col. Jack Potter [Santa Fe: Museum of New Mexico Press, 1980], 25-28. Burroughs includes several Potter tales told to NMFWP field writers.)

INDEX

58, 59, 62, 63, 64, 65, 67, 68, 69, 70, 71, 72, 77, 78, 79, 81, 82, 84, 88, 98, 99, 106
Lincoln County War, 8, 9, 10, 17, 20, 28, 29, 32, 41, 44, 62, 63, 65, 66, 80, 81, 102
Llano Estacado, N.M., 37
Long, Jack (John), 16, 17
Lopez, Julian, 72
Los Alamos, N.M., 43
Los Portales, N.M., 37
Luna, John, 34
Lynn, Bright, 42, 112

Mack Sween. *See* McSween, Alexander A.
Macky (McKee), Pedro, 75
Macky Nane (Thomas L. "Tip" McKinney), 68, 69
Macky Swin. *See* McSween, Alexander A.
MacMullen, John, 15
MacSain, Mrs. *See* McSween, Susan, Mrs.
Manning, Berta Ballard, 40
Manzano, N.M., 30, 31, 32, 62
Marfe. *See* Murphy, Lawrence G.
Martinez, Anastacio (Atanacio), 41, 42, 69
Martinez, Jose, Don, 104
Mason, Barney, 54, 107
Mathews, Jacob B. "Billy," 16, 17, 20, 22, 106
Maxwell, Deluvina, 90–91, 102
Maxwell, Lucien B., 90–91, 94, 97, 100, 121
Maxwell, Paulita, 78, 90–91
Maxwell, Peat. *See* Maxwell, "Pete"
Maxwell, "Pete" (Pedro), 36, 37, 78, 81, 85, 86, 90–91, 95, 96, 98, 100, 102, 121, 122
Mayer, Paul, 8, 81
McCarty, Catherine, 1, 4, 6, 8, 9, 10, 11, 12, 88, 103, 110, 111
McCarty, Joseph, 1, 2, 7
McCarty, Michael, 110
McClosky (William McCloskey), 68, 106
McKine (probably Thomas L. "Tip" McKinney), 88
McLoska. *See* McClosky
McNab, Frank, 20, 28, 106, 120
McSween, Alexander A., 17, 18, 19, 28, 29, 30, 31, 32, 34, 36, 62, 68, 69, 70, 71, 72, 76, 80, 81, 82, 88, 90–91, 102, 106
McSween (Barber), Susan, Mrs., 29, 32, 33, 34, 80, 90–91, 107
Meleton. *See* Middleton, John
Melton, John. *See* Middleton, John
Mescalero Agency, N.M., 105
Mescalero Apache Indian Reservation, N.M., 24
Mesilla, N.M., 57, 76, 78, 82, 89, 97
Middleton, John, 24, 25, 41, 42, 70, 71
Milton, John. *See* Middleton, John

Mimbres River, N.M., 13
Miranda, Emilio, 32
Miranda, Felipe, 32
Miranda, Jose Delores, 32, 34
Miranda, Lorencita, Mrs., 31
Mogollon Mountains, N.M., 45
Molina, Monocino, 28
Molina, Jose, 28
Montanies (Montaño) House, Lincoln, N.M., 102
Montoya, Jose, 41
Montoya, Lucio, 19, 20, 72
Moquesuin (McSween?), 37
Mora, 106
Morfes (Murphys), 37
Morton, William "Buck," 67, 68, 89, 106
Mote, Billy. *See* Morton, William "Buck"
Moulton, Ed, 2, 12, 117
Mowry City, N.M., 5
Murphy, Lawrence G., 36, 62, 67, 68, 69, 72, 73, 79, 88
Murphy-Dolan faction, 10, 17, 18, 19, 59, 102

O'Folliard, Tom (also spelled here O'Fallard, O'Fallered, O'Foillard), 19, 20, 29, 46, 49, 50, 86, 90–91, 97, 98, 105, 106
Ojo del Taiban, N.M. *See* Taiban, N.M.
Ojo Ranch, N.M., 69
Old Mesilla. *See* Mesilla, N.M.
Olinger, Robert "Bob" (also spelled here Ollenger and Ollinger), 10, 11, 22, 41, 42, 44, 57, 58, 59, 60, 62, 63, 83, 106, 117

Paden, M. G., Dr., 8, 43
Pajarito Canyon, N.M., 67
Pajarito Mountains, N.M., 17
Patron, Juan, 73, 102, 110
Pecos River, N.M., 36, 68, 69, 70, 94, 95, 98
Penasco, N.M., 67
Penfield Home and Store, Lincoln, N.M., 17, 21, 34
Peppin, George W. "Dad," 16, 17, 106
Picacho, N.M., 62, 69
Pierce Canyon, N.M., 57
Pino, Pablo, 17
Pinos Wells, N.M., 37
Poe, John William, 88, 90–91, 121
Poe, Mr., 87, 89
Poe, "Woodland," 107
Potter, Jack or John, 107, 108, 121, 122
Puerto de Luna, N.M., 46, 56, 75

Ragsdale, Katherine, 57, 113
Raines, Lester B., 38, 40, 113

125